THE ILLUSTRATED HISTORY OF
OFF-ROAD
VEHICLES

NICK BALDWIN

Foulis

Haynes

A **FOULIS** Motoring book

Published by:
Haynes Publishing Group
Sparkford, Nr. Yeovil, Somerset
BA22 7JJ, England

Haynes Publications Inc.
861 Lawrence Drive, Newbury Park,
California 91320 USA

**British Library Cataloguing in
Publication Data**

Baldwin, Nick
The illustrated history of off-road vehicles.
1. All terrain vehicles — History —
Pictorial works
I. Title
629.2'2042   TL209
ISBN 0-85429-614-X

Library of Congress catalog card number 87-82239

Editor: Robert Iles
Page layout: Tim Rose
Printed in England by: J.H. Haynes & Co. Ltd.

Contents

Introduction and Acknowledgements

Being just too young for National Service I missed the close involvement with off-road vehicles enjoyed, or at any rate tolerated, by so many servicemen since before the Second World War.

But for my father's close involvement with the Land-Rover at the Rover Co. Ltd., in the 1950s, I do not suppose I would have ever become an addict, but whilst other young men drooled over sportscars I became obsessed with off-road driving. Most weekends would find me with Ordnance Survey maps, ropes, shovel and my trusty Land-Rover somewhere in the Welsh border regions trying to reach some distant reference point across bogs and hills. I came to appreciate the ingenious engineering that goes into vehicles that can withstand repeated off-road use and began to study the other makes of vehicles that had four-, six- or even eight-wheel drive. I accumulated a great deal of material on the subject and this book has given me an extremely pleasant opportunity to sort through it and endeavour to trace the development of all-wheel drive and show some of the thousands of photographs that I have collected over the past thirty years. Unfortunately, I am unable to acknowledge the source of all the pictures, but to firms and individuals who have supplied them over the years I am most grateful. Special thanks should obviously go to my late father, and to the Land-Rover Owners' Club, from which has grown several off-road vehicle enthusiast groups including the AWDC. Thanks also to Bart Vanderveen, for helping to unravel the mysteries of military vehicles past and present when we both worked for *Old Motor* magazine, and to correspondents in several foreign countries too numerous to mention.

Finally, my special thanks to Nick Georgano and the late Michael Sedgwick, whose wide knowledge and interest in all forms of motorised transport helped me to broaden my outlook. Michael's catholic tastes are magnificently commemorated in the Michael Sedgwick Memorial Trust (Hon. Sec. B. Heath, Spring Cottage, 20 High Street, Milford on Sea, Lymington), which raises funds to publish books and pamphlets on the more obscure aspects of transport history. Luckily 4 x 4 has become a mainstream subject so does not require sponsorship of this sort, and thanks for this are due in part to my publishers, G.T. Foulis of the Haynes Publishing Group, who have made this book possible.

1 Cart tracks and Caterpillars

Vehicles able to travel without the need of roads or rails have fascinated inventors from the dawn of self-propulsion. After all, hard surfaced roads as opposed to cart tracks and droving ways, were extremely rare until the 1930s. Attempts were made in Victorian days to lower the ground pressure exerted by steam traction engines using ultra large wheels or else pads. In Paris, Gandon built a four-wheel-drive steam goods vehicle in 1900. Spyker of Amsterdam, Holland, built a 4 x 4 (four wheels x four driven) cars in 1904 and the forerunners of FWD built a small batch of 4 x 4 cars in Clintonville, Wisconsin, USA from 1908 before concentrating on trucks in 1912.

America had 2,151,379 miles of public roads in 1904 but only those in towns had hard surfaces. Out in the country they were just earth strips that turned into abrasive dust in the summer and quagmires in the winter. By 1914 3,296 miles had been hard surfaced. It was not until the Federal Aid Bill of 1921 that serious efforts were made to improve communications and by 1940 a million miles had been surfaced.

Roads were marginally more suitable for motor traffic in Europe, but conflict between nations was so commonplace that military vehicles able to traverse open country were high on the agenda of the motor industries of France, Austro-Hungary and Germany. In Britain, Standard supplied 4 x 4 light vehicles to the Delhi Durbah in 1913 and all manner of off-road 4 x 2s were built for the Colonies. The forerunners of Caterpillar in America made some gargantuan tracked vehicles before 1900 and Richard Hornsby in England applied the idea to various cars and steam vehicles in the early years of the century, which ultimately led to the tanks of the 1914/18 War.

Ferdinand Porsche developed an electric hub motor driven by a petrol powered generator in 1898 that greatly simplified applying power to steered wheels. Various petrol-electric 4 x 4s followed in the German and Austrian armies. Couple Gear and Quadray in America made electric 4 x 4s in 1904 and both followed up with gas-electrics.

Daimler Marienfelde made heavy 4 x 4 trucks with shaft drive from 1906, the year after Austro-Daimler started to make 4 x 4 gun tractors.

France and Italy were also making 4 x 4 tractors before the Great War, the former originally based on Latil front-wheel drive units.

Various British traction engine makers built machines employing James Boydell's track-laying wheel patents of 1846 and 1854. The first was built by Richard Bach of Birmingham in 1855 and this is a Burrell made in Thetford soon afterwards. As early as 1804 Oliver Evans in America had made a steam device said to be able to travel on land and water; numerous other inventors turned their minds to off-road mechanical transport as the nineteenth century progressed. The Boydell idea was revived by B. J. Diplock early this century using circular pads to create his Pedrail.

Off Road

Main photograph: **Col. Renard of the French Army developed a roadtrain in 1903 that differed from previous attempts in having driven trailer axles. Power was transmitted to one axle per trailer via a long universally jointed shaft that drove several trans-axles, each equipped with chain sprockets. The first was built by Darracq and an example was sold to Persia in 1904. English Daimler acquired a licence to build the machines in 1908 and here we see one in 1911 with an 80 hp 9.4 litre six-cylinder sleeve valve engine at work in Canada. Daimler soon abandoned the project, though Armstrong Whitworth made another type with petrol electric drive during the Great War.**

Opposite page top: Holt and Best made tractors in the 1890s with massive drive wheels to "float" on the fields of California. Benjamim Holt was the first to have a practical crawler, or as he called it, a caterpillar, at work in 1904. Here a 1908 example is demonstrated to some incredulous farmers. Note their horse-drawn "highweeler" buggy, the regular transport on rutted byways. Holt and Best combined in 1908, but a son, C.L. Best, started his own firm which merged with them in 1925 to form the Caterpillar Tractor Co.

From the horsedrawn "highwheeler" evolved a whole breed of similar motorised vehicles that could traverse the deeply rutted backroads of America. This is a Clark made in Lansing, Michigan in 1904 with opposed twin-cylinder air cooled 14 hp engine. Numerous other firms made similar cars and light commercials, amongst the best known of them being the International Harvester Co.

The snowy wastes of the Polar regions excited both explorers and motor manufacturers. De Dion-Bouton built this sledge, powered by an 1899-type air-cooled engine with the tiller steering column from an equally ancient car, for the 1908 French Antarctic Expedition. Ernest Shackleton used a 4 x 2 Arrol-Johnston vehicle on his Antarctic visit that year and in 1914 had another built by the same manufacturer with chain driven paddle wheels. Incidentally, Arrol-Johnston was involved with shipbuilding tycoon William Beardmore who was later to make Beardmore vehicles, and Shackleton named the Beardmore Glacier after him. Capt. Scott used fully tracked Wolseley sledge tractors in 1910, but none of these pioneer snow vehicles proved to be very successful.

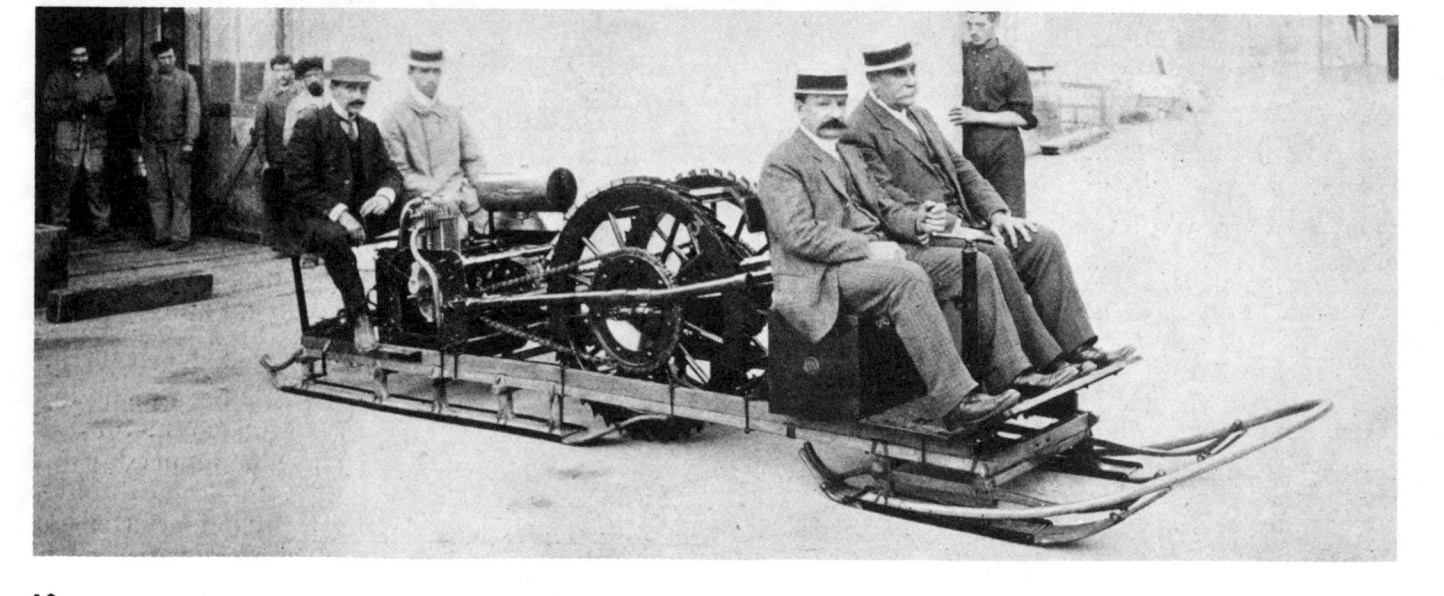

Below:
Though Britain was slow to make multi-wheel drive vehicles (the Delhi Durbah Standards and Daimler-Renard notwithstanding) it produced all manner of Colonial 4 x 2 cars, lorries and tractors around 1910. Principal features of the heavier ones were oversize radiators, giant metal straked drive wheels and power winches. Well known exponents were Broom and Wade, Halley, Dennis and Straker-Square. An example of the latter Bristol-based company's 5/6 tonner of 1912 is shown here. It had a drum on its back axle holding 50 yards of half inch diameter wire rope to help extricate it from tricky ground conditions. For the winch to be used independently the wheels had to be un-keyed from the axle!

Off Road

Between 1910 and 1912 the Caldwell Vale Motor and Tractor Construction Co. of Auburn, NSW, Australia, made some forty massive 4 x 4s with wheels of five feet diameter. They had four separately cast cylinders totalling more than eleven litres, three-speed gearboxes and power steering worked by chains and cone clutches. Many were used by the Government to provide road trains and at least one has survived into the vehicle preservation era.

A close up of the Caldwell Vale's differential casing (on left) with universal jointed drive shaft and steerings swivel. One of the front wheels is on the right and visible at the top of the picture is the road spring and power steering chain. Australia has had another indigenous maker of off-road vehicles, since 1969, namely RFW.

A Daimler Marienfelde 4 x 4 in 1909. Four and six-cylinder latter 60 bhp machines being supplied to Portuguese West had double reduction gearing to teeth in the wheel rims this otherwise largely conventional-looking chassis, shown versions were produced, one of the Africa in the same year. These Daimlers and the massive radius rods visible in here equipped with an anti-airship gun.

![Latil Levallois vehicle in mud at Fort Douaumont]

The French Latil concern was a pioneer of front-wheel drive in 1898. It made units that could be substituted for the front axle and turntable of horsedrawn vehicles. From there it was a relatively small step to power the rear wheels as well. Some had rear as well as front steering axles, including well over two thousand gun tractors built for the 1914/18 War. Here one is shown on test at Fort Douament, Verdun, in 1914. Panhard et Levassor, Balachowsky et Caire and Renault were other 4 x 4 producers at the time, the former offering all-wheel driven Chatillon-Panhards from 1911.

Ferdinand Porsche joined Austro-Daimler in 1905 in place of Paul Daimler, a son of the German motor pioneer Gottlieb Daimler. He remained there until 1923, making all manner of off-road vehicles. This is his four-cylinder overhead valve 13.5 litre 80 horsepower tractor of 1914 for towing 30.5 cms mortars. It had a three tonne winch, weighed almost ten tons and could attain 14.5 km/h. The wheels were 1.46 metres in diameter. In 1906 Austro-Daimler followed Coventry Daimler's example in separating from German Daimler's financial and technical influence.

Above:
As well as all-wheel driven vehicles the German industry made full and half-tracked off-road equipment. This photograph was originally captioned "Raupenschlepper der Daimler-Werke, 1910", but according to a similar machine shown in the Observer's Army Vehicles Directory to 1940, is in fact a Bussing Uberlandwagen of the Great War period, powered by twin Daimler four-cylinder 100 bhp engines. Load capacity was ten tons, or fifteen tons as a tractor. The carrier base was similar to the Daimler A7V tank.

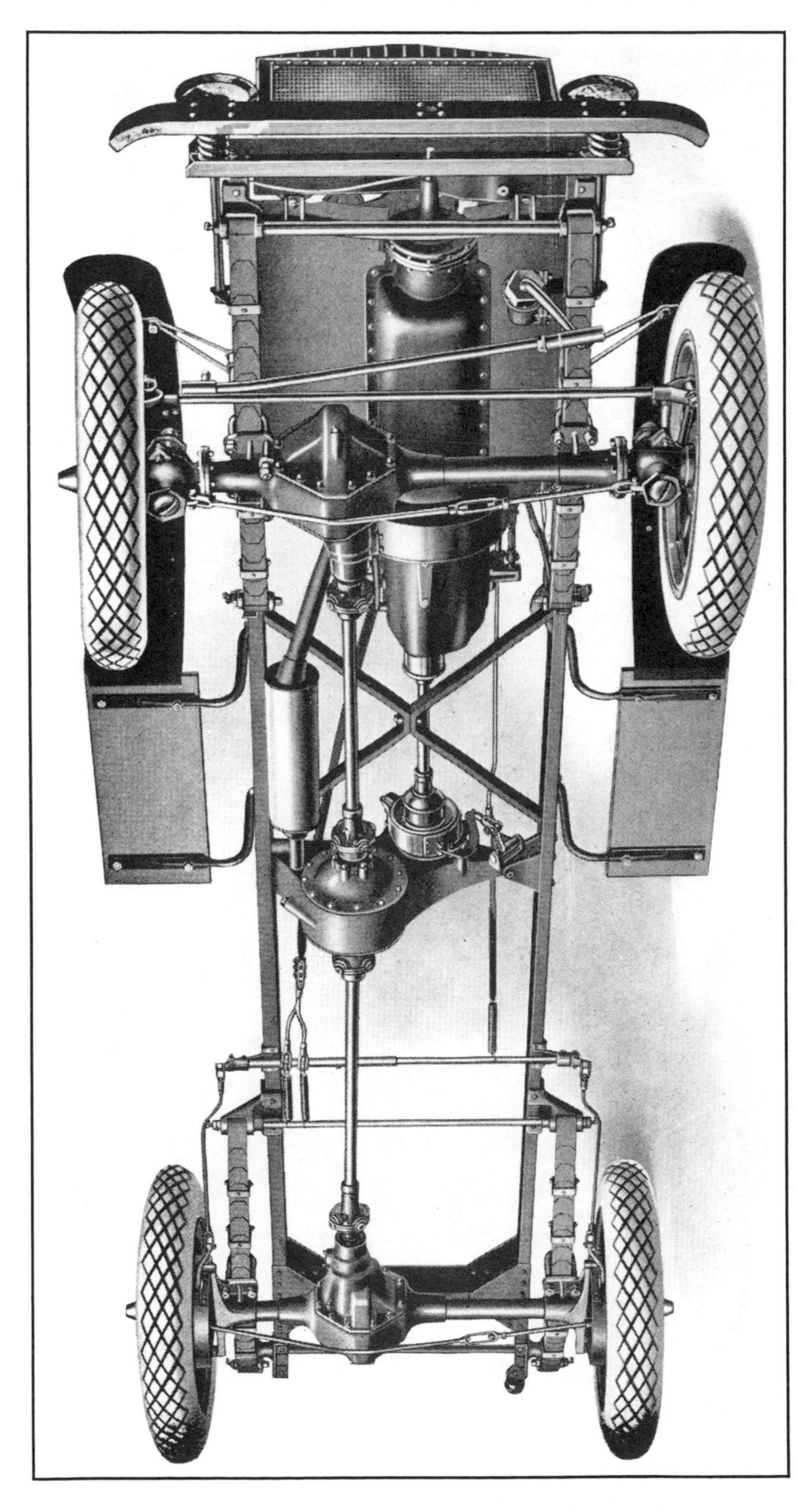

Opposite page bottom:
Zachow and Besserdich ran a machine shop in Clintonville, Wisconsin. Their 4 x 4 cars were initially Badgers, but changed their name following the creation of the Four Wheel Drive Auto Co. In 1911 they sold their first car; in 1912 six cars (including one to M. W. Pinkerton of detective agency fame) and five trucks, and in 1913 nineteen trucks. In 1914 they obtained an order for fifty army lorries from Britain and by the end of the War had made well over 10,000 FWD model B three tonners plus many more produced on their behalf by other manufacturers. The Model B had forward control and a 36 hp Wisconsin four-cylinder engine with three-speed constant mesh gearbox.

Left:
William Besserdich sold his shares in FWD in 1913 and departed with B.A. Mosling (who had actually bought many of his shares) to start a rival 4 x 4 business. It was originally called the Wisconsin Duplex Auto Co. of Clintonville but on its move to Oshkosh it became the Oshkosh Motor Truck Mfg. Co. in May 1917, when it built its first production trucks. These had Goodyear pneumatic tyres, when most rivals relied on solids, and an automatic third differential in the transfer case. Power came from a four-cylinder Herschell-Spillman 72 bhp petrol engine. Here we have a worm's eye view of a Model A Oshkosh showing a layout that has changed little on most 4 x 4 to the present day.

The lack of American roads and later the demands of the Great War saw numerous manufacturers tackle the 4 x 4 market. Amongst them were FWD, Oshkosh, Bulldog, Couple Gear who made an electric 4 x 4 in 1904 but later specialised in petrol (gas) -electrics, Quadray (electrics and gas-electrics in 1904/5), Militor (a Government-backed standardised wartime 4 x 4), Walter, Duplex (a Michigan based firm making 4 x 4s from 1908), Nash/Jeffrey and Winther. Shown here is a glimpse into the Oshkosh factory in 1919 and a completed Model A outside surrounded by the people who made it. Note the typical state of road which itself was far superior to what could be expected out in the country.

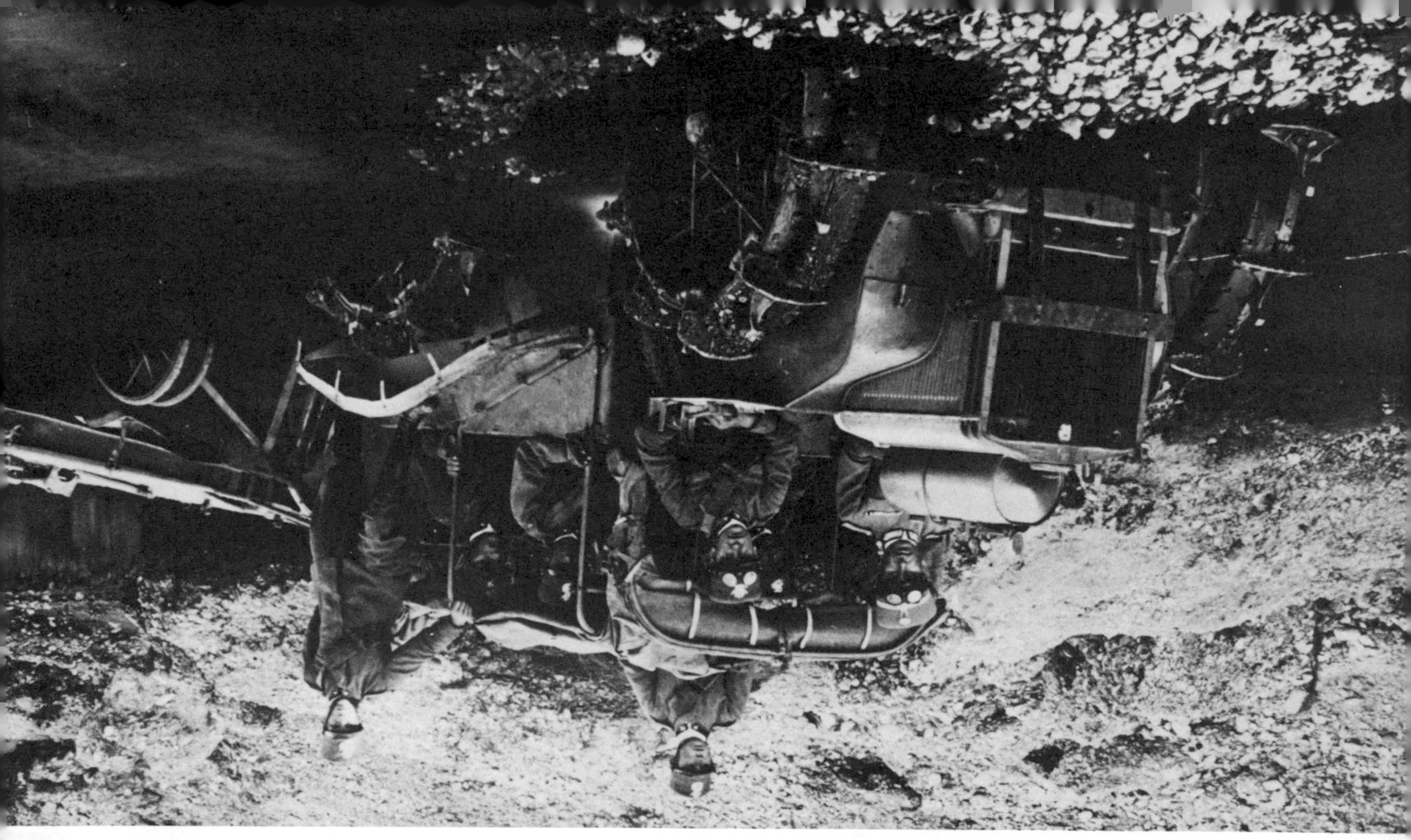

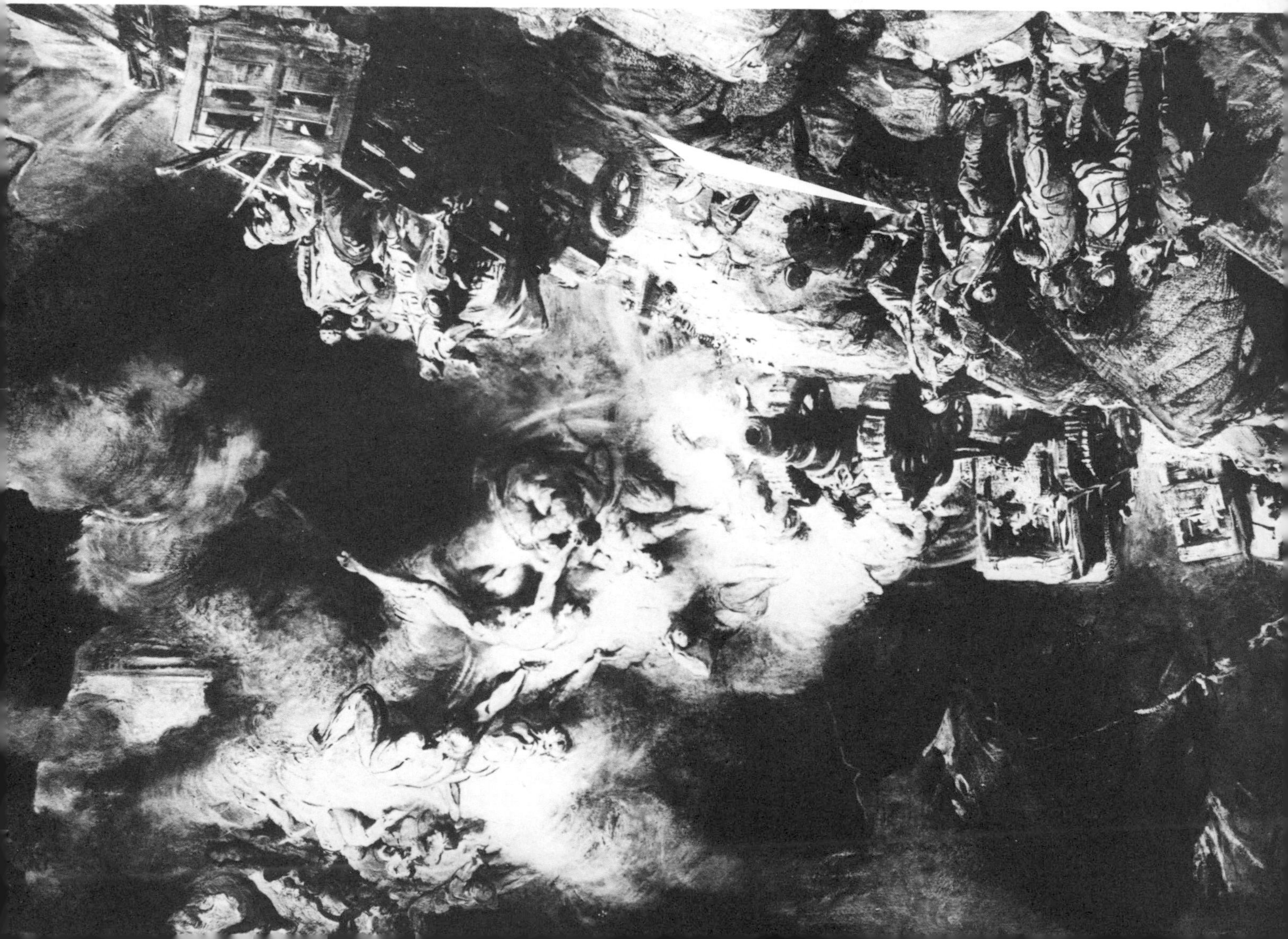

Opposite page top: A highly glorified view of warfare from a FIAT poster of the 1914/18 period. FIAT had made its first specifically designed gun tractor in 1909. During the war it made some of the massive 10.6 litre 60 bhp machines depicted in the centre with Bonagente tracks that lozenged over the rear wheels to increase traction and reduce ground pressure. FIAT was later to take over most of the other Italian producers of off-road vehicles, including Ceirano, Pavesi, Spa and latterly Lancia.

Above: An interesting view of a 1915 Lanchester chassis used as the basis for armoured cars, ambulances and cargo vehicles. Made by a pioneer Birmingham motor company that was ultimately to join the BSA/Daimler group, Lanchesters bristled with unusual technical features. This one had epicyclic transmission, a six-cylinder 38 hp motor, double cantilever rear springs and coil spring front suspension. The twin rear tyres were filled with an elastic compound called Rubberine instead of air. As yet Britain was not producing more than the odd experimental 4 x 4, and the British Quad with Dorman engine did not get into quantity production.

Left: The Pavesi was an ingenious 4 x 4 with two-way pivots between the front and rear portions that allowed the machine to steer and keep all its wheels in equal contact with the ground. Designed by Ing Pavesi during the 1914/18 War, when many of his 4 x 4 gun tractors were in use, it was built initially (like the one shown) by SA La Motomeccanica, but from 1926 by FIAT. To begin with the Pavesi had a flat twin-cylinder engine but soon grew up in size and power. Similar compact 4 x 4 machines but without the pivot frames were made between the wars by OM, Breda, Alfa Romeo and Spa.

Like the FWD, Winther and Oshkosh, the Jeffery (originally Rambler) Quad hailed from the state of Wisconsin. It was made from 1913 to 1916, when the factory was sold to Charles W. Nash and the Quad became a Nash Quad from the 1918 model season. For $1^1/2$-2 ton loads the Quad resembled the Latil, in having both 4 x 4 and four-wheel steering. Power came from a Buda 36 horsepower engine. Here we have an early example in use with the US Army Signal Corps as a "radio tractor". 5,578 Rambler Quads were made in the first season and 11,490 in its first year as a Nash. Hudson National and Paige also built them under licence.

Top right: One could almost call this the Land-Rover or Jeep of its day. Thousands of these Manchester built Crossley 4 x 2 chassis with twin rear tyres for extra traction, were built during the 1914/18 War. They were the basis of ambulances, staff cars and $^3/4$ ton cargo tenders. This example has a 20/25hp $4^1/2$ litre four-cylinder engine. Crossley retained close links with the services between the wars, supplying many 6 x 4 cross-country chassis, followed by 4 x 4 lorries during the Second World War.

Opposite page: A British advertisement dating from June 1915 for the Quad. The importers also represented FWD in Europe. Thomas Jeffery had started as a maker of Rambler bicycles in 1879 and had added cars this century. He died in 1910 and was succeeded by his son Charles, who sold out to Nash just before the bubble burst and 4 x 4s were no longer needed for the war effort. Charles Nash had been president of Buick and then of General Motors. Nash Motors eventually became a cornerstone of American Motors and therefore is a direct antecedent of the Jeep. A former Jeffery employee made the rival Winther-Marwin (later Winther-Kenosha) 4 x 4 also in Kenosha for ten years from 1917.

2 From the First World War ...

The decade following the First World War saw all manner of ex-WD vehicles, including FWDs and Quads, coming onto the second-hand market. These widened the experience of operators but decimated the factories attempting to sell new vehicles. FWD, Oshkosh, Duplex and Walter survived in America by becoming much more specialist and producing smaller numbers of fully equipped vehicles for such duties as snow ploughing, road maintenance, power line riggings and oilfield duties.

In Europe re-armament was slow, but when it did take place it was light 6 x 4 vehicles that appealed most, at any rate to the British and French authorities. Nearly all civilian requirements for 4 x 4 and 6 x 6 vehicles were met by British FWD, which had grown out of a reconditioning business at Slough and would eventually inspire AEC to make the Matador 4 x 4. Scammell also gained importance, but it was the light 6 x 4s that sold in the greatest numbers. Most popular of all was the Morris-Commercial D type, introduced in 1927, that accounted for 4,400 sales over the next six years.

As well as a massive growth of interest in 6 x 4 vehicles there was a major revival of the half-track idea. This had existed since the early years of the century but came into its own in the 1920s. Christie Crawlers in America, Kégresse in France and Roadless in Britain were some of the best known names. Many existing vehicles were converted, though thousands of new Citroen-Kégresse vehicles were built for roles later to be taken over by light 4 x 4s. Temporary tracks were also evolved for fitting over the rear bogies of six wheelers that worked only occasionally in impassable conditions.

Everywhere the need to open up under-developed countries and exploit their natural resources led to a major growth in off-road transport.

Opposite page:
A pair of Holt Caterpillars pulls an enormous wagon train across the Mohave Desert during the construction of the Los Angeles Aqueduct. 75 bhp four-cylinder and 120 bhp six-cylinder Holts of this sort had been supplied in large numbers as gun tractors during the 1914/18 War. Numerous other half-track vehicles had been built since the turn of the century, including what were effectively steam railway locomotives on tracks with wheels or sledges for steering. These were used for timber extraction in North America.

Top: Lt. Col. Philip Johnson, head of Britain's Tank Design and Experimental Dept started Roadless Traction Ltd at Hounslow in 1919. In the next thirty years he was to put all manner of unlikely machines onto full or half tracks. He started, appropriately enough, with an Overland car on tracks and soon progressed to farm tractors and even steam wagons. Shown here is an Austin Twenty equipped as a cross country load and personnel carrier in the early 1920s.

The Royal Army Service Corps made this Hathi (Hindusthani for elephant) in 1922/3 from captured German components. They then laid down a specification on which Thornycroft based about two dozen more Hathis, including at any rate one 6 x 6. The Thornycroft versions used 11.2 litre six-cylinder 90 bhp marine engines and were supplied for military and civilian use at home and overseas. They had two range, three-speed gearboxes that also provided two reverse ratios and were fitted with 13 ton capacity winches. Thornycroft was to have greater commercial success with 6 x 4 military and colonial chassis.

Off Road

Insets: In Sweden Scania-Vabis had built 4 x 4 fire engines during the Great War as well as an enormous experimental 4 x 4 load carrier and tractor (the front wheel and cab of which are just visible behind the 6 x 4 on test in 1922/3). However, its 1920s efforts were limited to half-track post buses and semi-off road 6 x 4 types. The post-buses had four-speed gearboxes with an additional high/low ratio gearbox on the back axle. They carried passengers in the saloon with the mail on a sledge or trailer behind. The 6 x 4 types were for 3 and 6 ton loads with double reduction axles and had overhead valve engines from 1924.

Main photograph: The Kégresse-Hinstin "endless band driving attachment" was a similar idea to the half-tracks being developed by Christie in America and Roadless in Britain. Monsieur Kégresse had been manager of Czar Nicholas II's garage. He had been instrumental in fitting a Rolls-Royce Silver Ghost with tracks whilst in Russia and on his return to France had collaborated with Citroen, which in a few years from 1919 had become Europe's largest producer of cars. Thousands of Citroen-Kégresse vehicles were built following the successful conquering of the Sahara by a team of 20 bhp examples in 1922. This feat was soon followed by the Black Expedition (shown here) from Algeria to Capetown and Madagascar.

These four and the following page top photograph: A random assortment of some of the early vehicles that Roadless put on tracks. The one wading out of a pond is an AEC 501, whilst the lorry with canvas cab and tilt is a Peugeot. The curious little articulated machine with wheels for steering and stability is based on Morris-Commercial components as used in the Martel Tankette. The steam tractor is a Sentinel and the lorry marked APOC (Anglo Persian Oil Co.) is a Morris-Commercial. Most Roadless load carriers were based on the cheap and robust 1 ton Morris-Commercial, a model that had first appeared in 1924.

These three and opposite page bottom: **As the 1920s progressed it was 6 x 4 rather than 4 x 4 vehicles that most British manufacturers supplied for off-road use. The War Department had patented a central trunnion-mounted rear suspension that allowed very considerable wheel articulation and the design was freely available to the British motor industry. Most resultant vehicles ranged in capacity between 1½ and 3 tons and a selection is shown here along with a 1924 4 x 2 Albion 1½ tonner on pneumatic tyres. This was a *subsidy* type, which meant that the operator could claim a form of rental in exchange for keeping it in good condition for possible military service. The six-wheelers are a Thornycroft with tyre chains, a Morris-Commercial D type in a ford and a forward control Karrier. Other makers of similar vehicles included Vulcan (who also tried a few 4 x 4s in 1926), Garner, Crossley, Guy and even Trojan who made a tiny 1.5 litre six-wheeler in 1929 able to carry ten men.**

Off Road

Walter built its first 4 x 4 in New York in 1911. William Walter was a Swiss immigrant who had started by producing machinery for making chocolates and built himself a car in 1898. Trucks were sold from 1909 and until 1920 used Walter's own engines. The Snow Plow Tractor shown here probably had a Waukesha petrol motor. The same chassis was used for various off-road roles as well as for snow fighting. The gross weight of the truck, trailer and load in this 1925 photograph is 61 tons.

In the first chapter we saw an early Pavesi tractor. As well as being adopted by FIAT in Italy, several foreign manufacturers produced machines incorporating its patents. These are the Armstrong-Siddeley versions as displayed at the London Commercial Motor Show stand in 1929. They had four-cylinder air cooled petrol engines, lockable differentials, pivoting frames and epicyclic four-speed self-changing gearboxes, the latter an Armstrong-Siddeley speciality more normally found on its luxury cars. In 1929 Armstrong-Siddeley also built an 8 x 8 version powered by one of its Genet five-cylinder radial aero engines.

Load carriers with full tracks were made in several countries during the 1920s. In Britain they were particularly for military requirements. Vickers-Armstrong were well known in this field with the Carden-Loyd $1\frac{1}{2}$ tonner from 1928. A broadly similar vehicle is shown here in the shape of the Gefrat made in Berlin around 1930. An unusual feature of it was that the tracks could bend two dimensionally and so actually steered. This was claimed to minimise track wear on hard surfaces.

Off Road

Chenard-Walcker made 4 x 2 road tractors from 1919 in Paris and in the late 1920s added off-road 6 x 4 versions. The one shown here had a sleeve valve Panhard engine, a winch behind the cab and was capable of towing twelve tons. A more powerful version in 1931 had twin engines side by side totalling 250 bhp. The individual tracks over each set of double rear wheels could be removed for road travel.

Below and opposite page:
In America thousands of surplus wartime 4 x 4s had been pressed into service by the government to aid a massive road building programme. The market for new 4 x 4s was very depressed and firms like FWD stayed in business by supplying spares and maintenance advice. In Britain, a firm in Slough reconditioned FWDs and, as original parts ran out, various locally sourced components were substituted. In 1927 a 6 x 6 FWD England appeared. To begin with it had a Dorman engine but, following its maker's links with AEC in 1929, it adopted the latter's six-cylinder power units. To avoid confusion with American FWD the marque under AEC ownership became known as Hardy in 1931. The R6T was produced by AEC/Hardy as the 850 model to 1936. The diagrams date from 1927 and show different FWD models and their off-road capabilities.

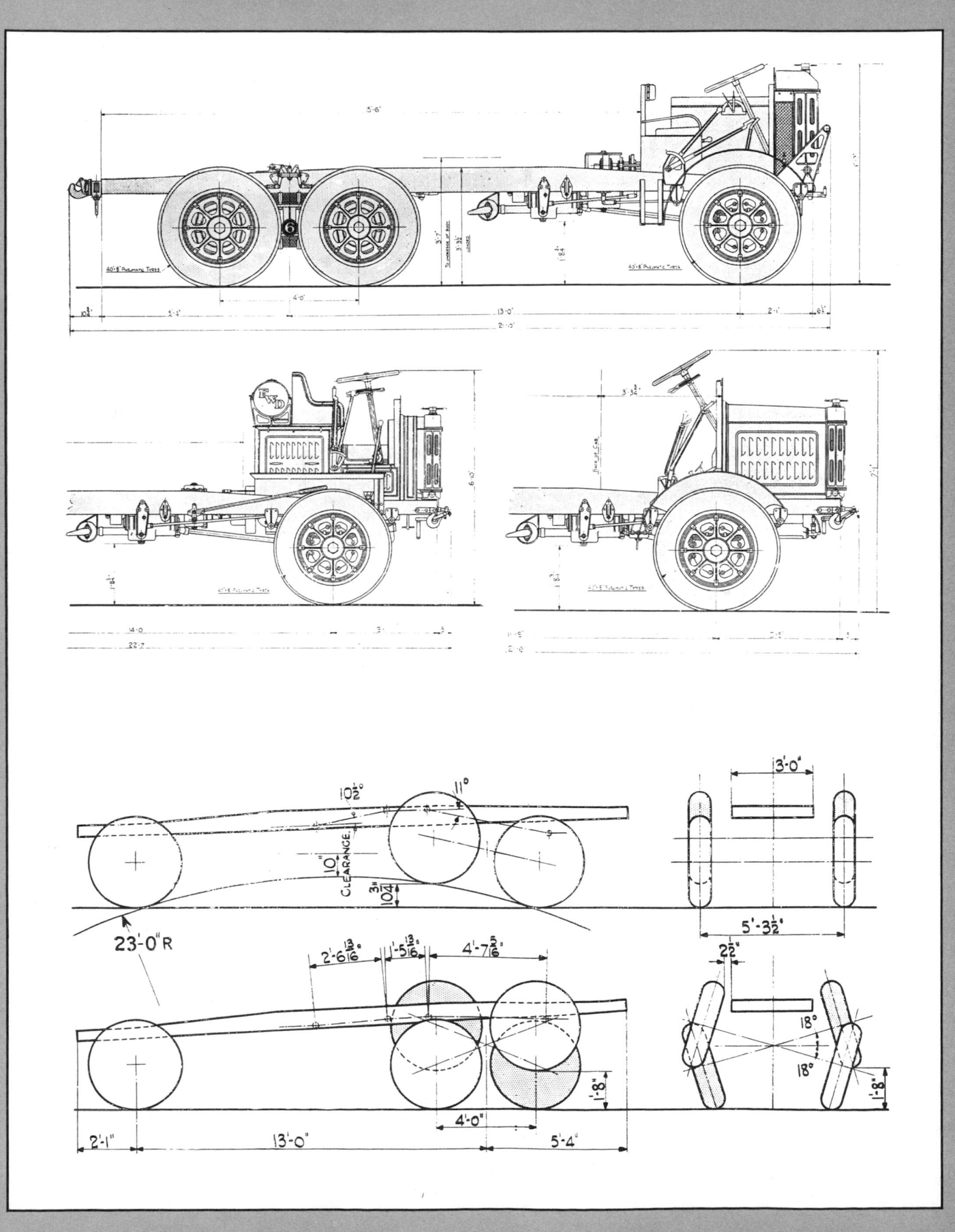

The French Kégresse track system was used by Crossley and Burford in Britain as well as by Citroen, who established a British factory at Slough. Here we see a Burford two tonner as supplied to the Empire Cotton Growing Corporation in the mid 1920s. It had a two-range, four-speed gearbox and a 5.13 litre petrol engine and could haul a six ton trailer. H.G. Burford had imported American Fremont-Mais trucks under his own name since 1914 and had also sold American Cletrac tractors as Burford-Cletracs. His trucks became increasingly British in the 1920s and disappeared in the 1930s after being taken over by Lacre.

Photographs on opposite page: One of the most famous names in off-road vehicles became Scammell of Watford after the introduction of its 6 x 4 Pioneer in 1927. Within two years it could be supplied with 6 x 6 as shown here. A centrally pivoted transverse front leaf spring and walking beam rear suspension permitted a remarkable degree of wheel movement. The engine was Scammell's usual 65 bhp 7 litre petrol unit. The head-on view shows an example with "coffee pot" radiator header tank to ensure that water remained above the tubes at whatever angle the vehicle was working.

Off Road

FIAT made this 1014 model in 1929 using a 1350 cc four-cylinder 28 bhp petrol engine to propel it and its half ton load. The centre and rear axle were driven and an articulated joint allowed the trailer to move laterally and vertically. It was geared to a top speed of 18 or 25 mph depending on axle ratios and could climb a gradient of 1 in 1$\frac{1}{2}$.

This strange vehicle is included more because of who made it than what it is. Robert G. LeTourneau envisaged vehicles on a grander scale than all his American contemporaries, save perhaps Holt and Best (Caterpillar). In the 1950s his firm made giant land trains and forest clearers and its Haulpak dumptrucks are still in production. Shown is LeTourneau's idea for a self-powered earth scraper in 1923. It had a transversely mounted petrol engine which powered electric wheel motors as well as the scraper.

3 The Growth Years

The 1930s marked a time of considerable growth in off-road transport. In Britain a Colonial Committee came up with an 8 x 8 road train specification to open up undeveloped territories. In the Middle East oil exploration was mushrooming and all sorts of vehicles were developed for carrying drilling equipment in the desert. Overlying all these peaceful pursuits was the re-armament that gathered pace from the middle of the decade.

Two important developments in America were the arrival of cheap Ford-based cross country vehicles from Marmon-Herrington in 1936 and purpose-built earthmovers from Euclid two years earlier.

In Germany, which had appreciated the advantages of all-wheel drive for longer than almost any other country, a new lighter breed of 4 x 4 car evolved.

In America, Bantam, which had made the Austin Seven under licence, made a similar style of vehicle which was to become the immortal Jeep of the 1940s.

Guy Motors of Wolverhampton had a thriving trade in military and colonial vehicles. They developed a heavy 6 x 6 in the late 1920s from which evolved the 8 x 8 shown here on test in 1931. Both had 96 bhp six-cylinder petrol engines and two range, four-speed transmissions, which gave 1.35 mph in low/low ratio at maximum power and 23 mph in high/high. There were conventional worm driven rear axles but the front ones were driven by two separate propeller shafts running down the outside of the chassis to worm gears and then final reduction in the wheel hubs. Other 8 x 8 vehicles were tried at the time or soon afterwards by various manufacturers, including Morris-Commercial, AEC, Leyland, Mercedes-Benz, Latil, MAN and Saurer.

Off Road

Main photograph:

A Scammell Pioneer 6 x 4 hauls a load of tree trunks in the sort of territory for which it was designed. Scammell's famous designer, O.D. North, was responsible for a wide assortment of off-road vehicles in the 1930s, including 6 x 6 armoured cars with radial engines and 4 x 4 tractors (also 4 x 2 types with oversize chain driven driving wheels). From 1933 most employed Gardner diesel engines, whose low revs and massive torque suited the character of the vehicles. They made an ideal replacement for Scammell's long running four-cylinder petrol engine, rated at 40 hp by the RAC, that continued to be offered right through the 1930s and was popular with export customers.

Inset photographs:

Medium capacity, normal control 6 x 4 models continued to be popular with the British military authorities in the 1930s, but less so with civilian hauliers who preferred maximum capacity diesel forward-control four wheelers for normal haulage duties that could carry the same seven ton payload at less cost than the petrol engined Albions shown here. However, for specialist roles, where the advantages of double drive outweighed initial cost, 6 x 4 still ruled supreme. This six-cylinder 43.4 RAC horsepower tipper was used for bulding an underground hangar and factory at Staverton and had temporary over tracks for the rear bogey when the ground became particularly soft. The forward control Albion shown on the firm's test track in 1930 was one of a number supplied to the government of India.

Opposite page top:

In 1932, when this 72,000 lbs gross weight outfit was built by FWD in America, the demand for 4 x 4 trucks was still relatively low. FWD had recently supplied 120 similar 4 x 4 rigids to the US Army with 127 bhp Waukesha petrol engines, but with the General Slump at its height there were few orders for utility trucks, and thousands of old B-types were still in active use anyway. With this conventional highway unit FWD hoped to appeal to long distance hauliers who wanted to keep to schedule in snowy conditions or whose routes took them off the major state highways. Few transport men availed themselves of the extra costs and complexities of 4 x 4.

Above and left:

Major civil engineering projects in America around 1930 encouraged the development of a new breed of heavy duty truck for carrying boulders, ore and overburden. Hug, Mack, and others developed special dumptrucks and in 1934 they were joined by a new make, Euclid, which was a division of an established crane manufacturer. Known as the Euclid Trac-Truk its vehicles could be 4 x 2 rigids or artics. Shown are artic bottom dumps and a 1934 rear dump with temporary tracks over its drive wheels, partly to protect the pneumatic tyres from sharp rocks. The Euclid business still exists today having been through the hands of numerous owners, including General Motors, White, Daimler-Benz and Clark (Michigan). Details of the many dumptrucks available at the time can be found in Nick Baldwin's book "Giant Dumptrucks" available in this series.

Off Road

The following six photographs: A major newcomer to the American scene was the Indianapolis based Marmon-Herrington Inc. in 1931. Col. Arthur W. Herrington had been involved with off-road vehicles in the Army and put all he had learned, plus his excellent contacts, to good use. Marmon-Herringtons were particularly successful in America and the Middle East. To begin with most had Hercules or Cummins engines, but from 1936 a speciality became off-road conversions of Ford vehicles, though the heavy vehicles continued. Here we have an assortment, including a 1934-pattern armoured car, an oil well cementing lorry operated by Earle Halliburton in the early 1930s, a 6 x 6 wrecker, a 6 x 6 tractor with mobile workshop semi-trailer, a Ford-based half track with driven front axle (apparently for the first time on a tracked vehicle in America) and finally a view of the factory showing Mead Morrison winches being fitted. After the War Marmon-Herrington became better known for buses but a descendant, Marmon Transmotive, still offers all-wheel drive conversions of commercial chassis and another, the Marmon Motor Co, makes on-highway "ten wheelers".

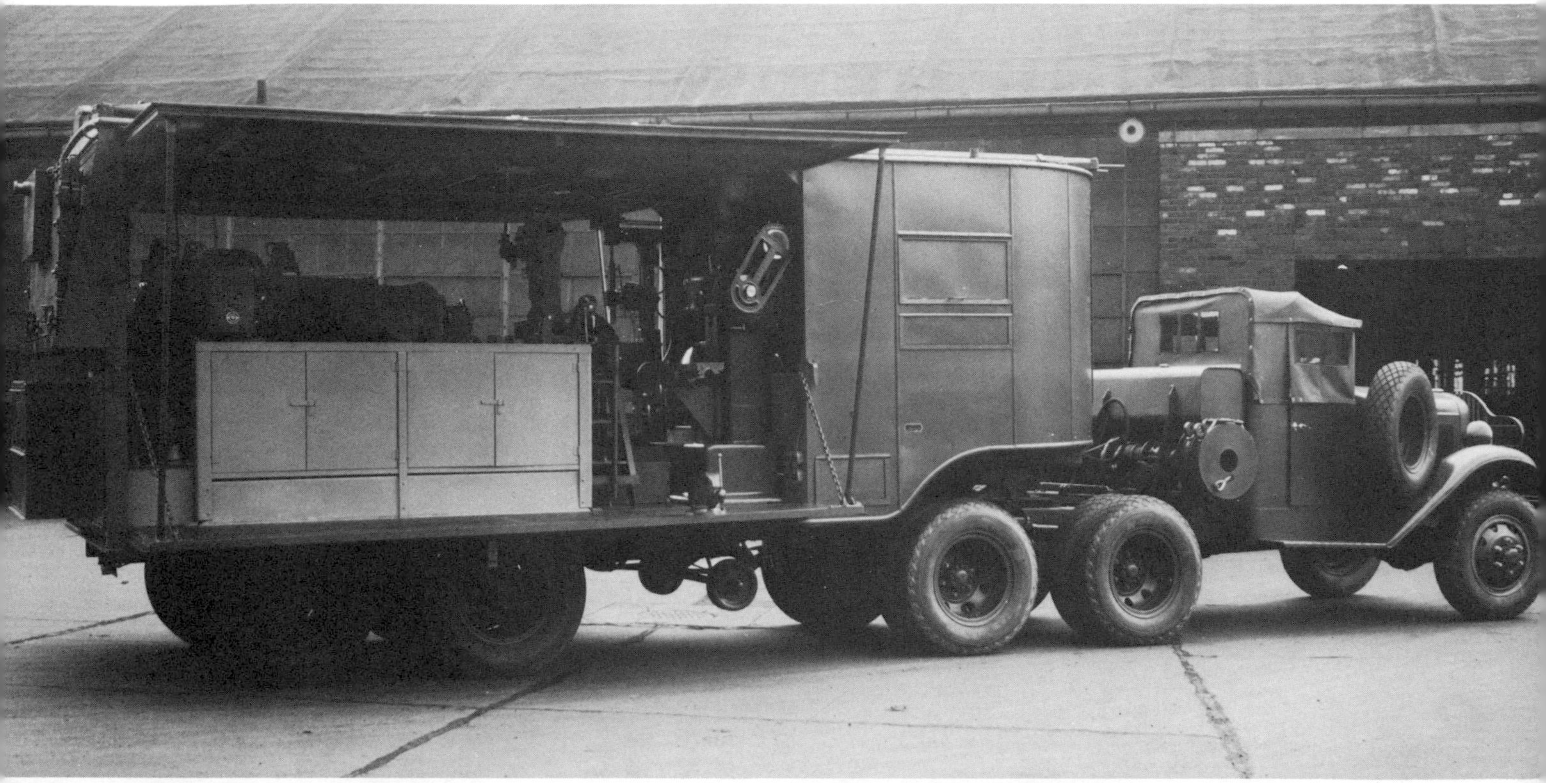

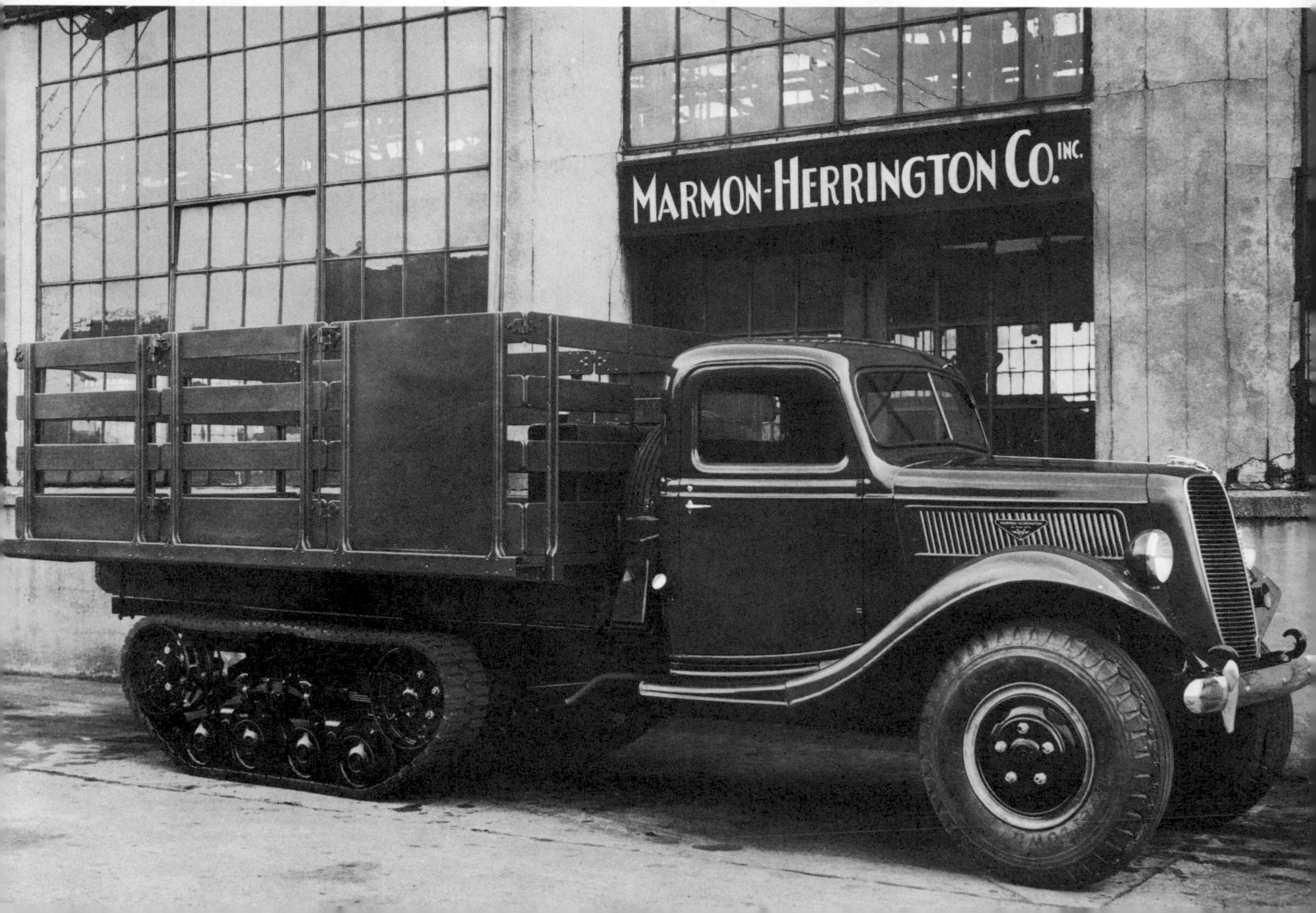
MARMON-HERRINGTON CO. INC.

After his two epic journeys by Citroen-Kégresse in the 1920s, Georges-Marie Haardt set out again with 39 companions in 1931 to traverse Asia. This time seven larger Citroens, two of which are shown here, drove from Peking through the Gobi desert to the foothills of the Himalayas whilst lighter models headed from Beirut, through Afghanistan and as far as they could get in the Himalayas – the remaining distance to be covered by pack animal. The journey was unbelievably arduous for both machines and men. Haardt, a Citroen factory manager of many years standing, died of double pneumonia in Hong Kong on the return journey. The Citroens had some very narrow escapes. For example, one fell through the ice of the Yellow River and another was left hanging over a 600 foot drop when a mountain path collapsed.

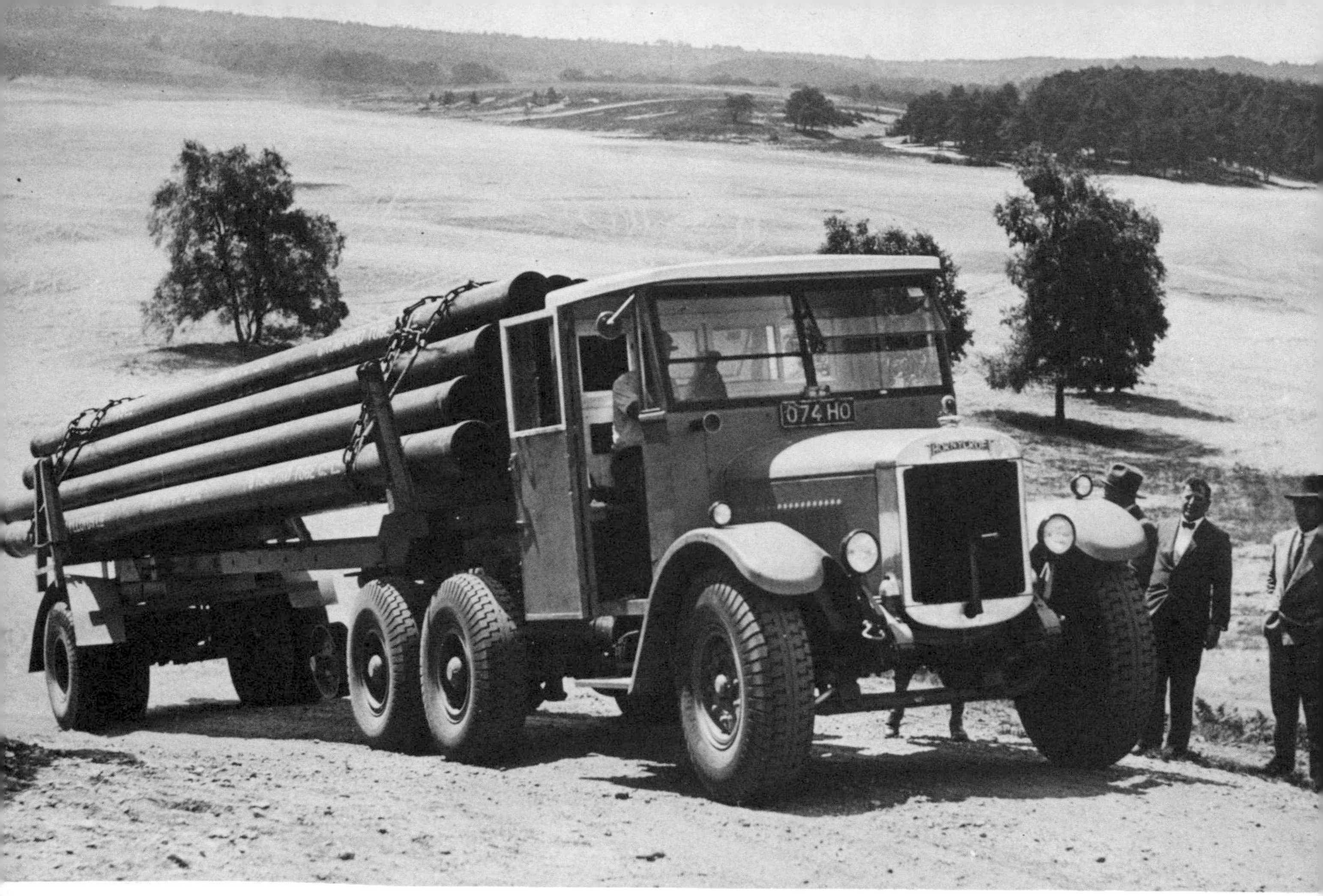
074 HO
THORNYCROFT

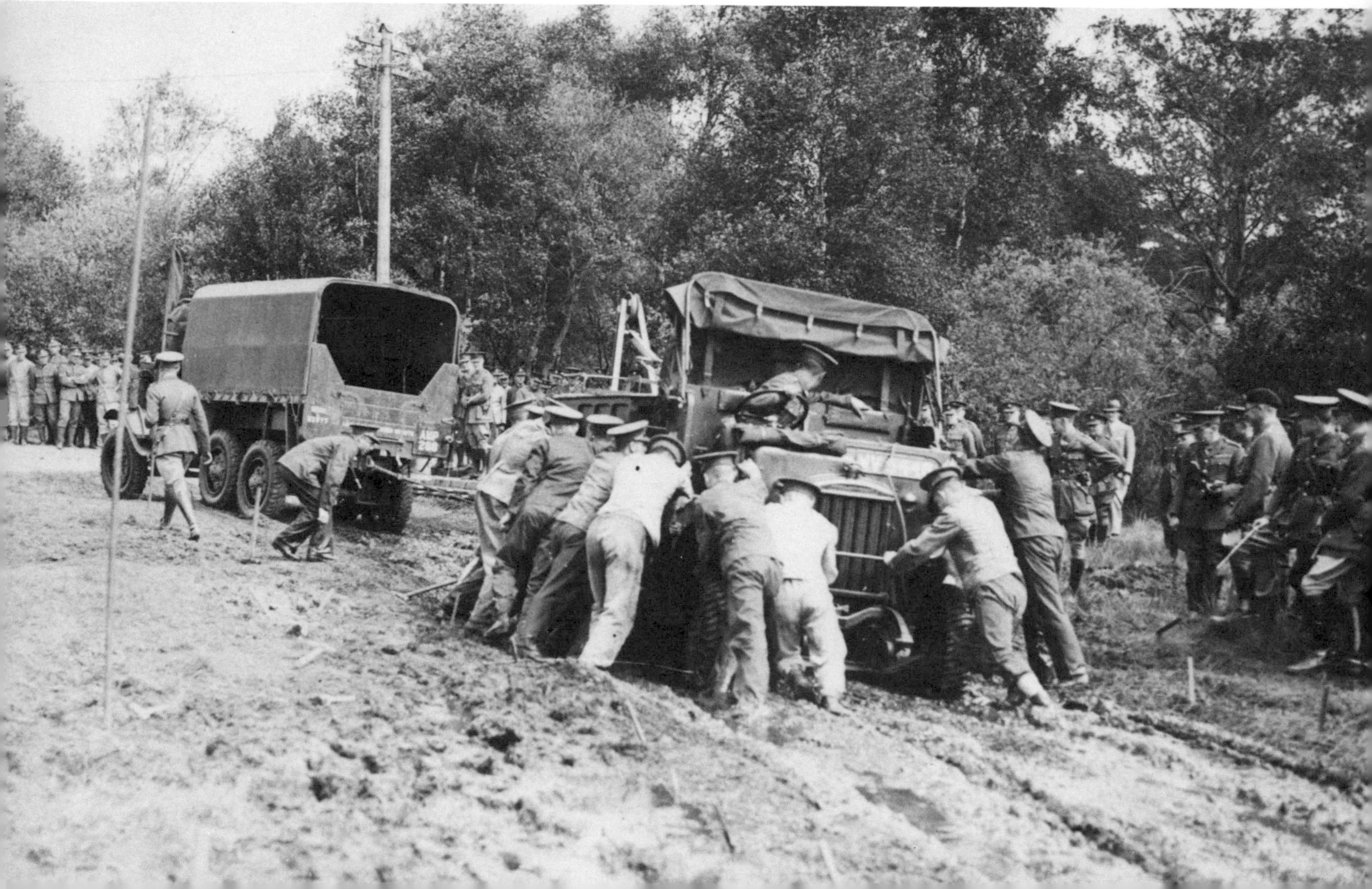

Right and opposite page:
Here we see three typical British 6 x 4s on trial. The Thornycroft was destined for the Anglo-Iranian Oil Co. in 1938 and is shown on the military proving grounds at Bagshot. The vehicle stuck in the mud is a forward control version of the Morris-Commercial D type during military manoeuvres. It is being rescued by a newer Morris-Commercial CD of the mid 1930s. The bonnetted six-wheeler with over-tracks is an AEC Marshal 644, a four to five tonner which had a 31 RAC horsepower four-cylinder petrol engine and was new in 1932.

When AEC acquired FWD England in 1929 it also gained a subsidiary called Hardy Rail Motors, which had built versions of FWD with flanged wheels. To avoid confusion with American FWD all the 4 x 4 and 6 x 6 trucks became known as Hardy from 1932 and this is its 4/4 four tonner of 1933. As can be seen, it is broadly similar in appearance to a contemporary AEC and had a 65 bhp four-cylinder AEC petrol or diesel engine with two range transfer box.

Above:

At the Colonial Office conference of 1927, 23 countries agreed to share the cost of a road train suitable for use in undeveloped countries. Shown here is AEC's answer to the problem in 1933. It was a 130 bhp 8 x 8 machine that towed two Dyson trailers each with four axles. The combined payload on the 71'8" long outfit was 15 tons, which could be transported at up to 28 mph. Naturally much FWD/Hardy expertise was incorporated in the design, which used two bogies from the Marshall cross country chassis on the tractor with the first and last axle modified to be able to steer. Several of these impressive units were built, going as far afield as Africa, Russia and Australia.

Above right:

One of the most original designers of off-road vehicles in the 1930s was Nicholas Straussler from Hungary. He brought several designs to Britain that were then worked on by Alvis and Garner. Shown is a vehicle that began life at the Manfred Weiss factory in Budapest. About fifty were built by Garner in North London from 1938, their most unusual feature being the twin Ford V8 petrol engines. These both drove back into a transfer box from which prop shafts emerged in the normal way. Thus the vehicles could be driven on one or two engines, depending on load and ground conditions.

48

Below: Czechoslovakia had several producers of 4 x 4 and 6 x 6 vehicles in the 1930s, notably Skoda, Praga and Tatra. The most interesting technically was the Tatra designed by Hans Ledwinka with a central backbone chassis, swing axle bogie and independent front suspension. Several versions were made, the one shown being a T85 current between 1936 and 1938. It was powered by an 8.2 litre four-cylinder 80 bhp petrol engine with two range four-speed gearbox. From 1939 Tatras used air cooled diesels. After the War Ledwinka was imprisoned by the new communist regime for having collaborated with the Germans in making military vehicles.

Walter, like Oshkosh and FWD, made 4 x 4 snowplough, load hauling and road maintenance trucks in the 1930s. Walter differed from the others in its Four Point Positive Drive, which was similar to the Latil system in featuring dead axles (without vulnerable diff. banjos) with drive fed into the hub reduction gearing by separate shafts that carried none of the load. The torque proportioning differentials also contained inboard mounted brakes out of the way of grit and water. These 1937/8 examples all had 150 bhp engines and six-speed gearboxes.

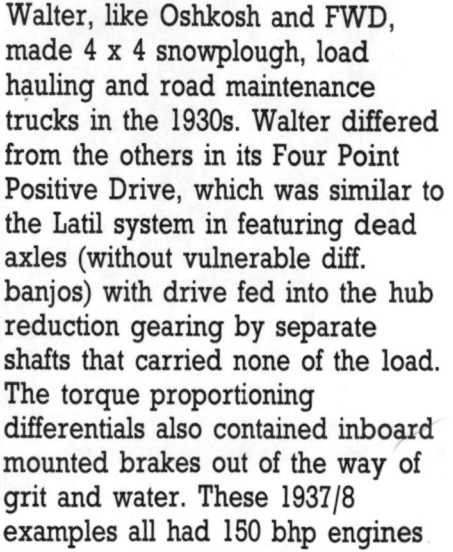

Guy switched almost totally to military vehicle production in 1936. Amongst its production was the ³/₄ ton Ant 4 x 2 and armoured car, which was a pioneer user of welded armoured steel – a process that Guy presented free of charge to the War Department. Humber mass-produced the armoured car during the Second World War. The Ant was available as the 4 x 4 Quad-Ant from 1937 and both types employed 50 bhp Meadows overhead valve four-cylinder petrol engines.

OM inherited the Cappa designed Autocarretta from Ansaldo in 1932 and a year later was itself acquired by FIAT. The Autocarretta da Montagna had a two-cylinder air-cooled 1.6 litre engine developing 21 bhp. It had four-wheel drive with lockable differentials, four-wheel steering and all-round independent suspension. Later FIAT and Spa were to make larger but similar vehicles that had plainly inherited many design features from the OM.

4 The War and after

This chapter covers the 1940s, a decade in which the most significant event was the Second World War. Much has appeared in print about the military vehicles of this period so we will do no more than show a few of the more significant vehicles.

The return to peace at the end of 1945 brought many similar problems for the motor industry that had faced it at the end of the 1914/18 War. Thousands of orders evaporated overnight and a flood of ex-military vehicles soon came on the market. Many of them, particularly Scammells, Diamond Ts and Matadors are still at work today in such civilian roles as vehicle recovery and logging. For an appreciable period there was very little demand for new off-road vehicles, one notable exception however being the Land-Rover of 1948. At the time the British motor factories were being exhorted to export and receiving steel in direct proportion to their success. Rover had never been a significant exporter, but was to change all that by using Birmabright aluminium alloy for its Land-Rover based on the concept of the legendary Jeep of the Second World War.

The Jeep, a corruption of "general purpose" (GP), was developed by Karl Probst at the American Bantam Car Co. Bantam made 2,675 in all, but could not keep pace with demand and the contract to mass-produce similar vehicles was split between Ford and Willys-Overland. Here we see a Ford helping to increase food production in England's West Country in 1943. It had a 54 bhp four-cylinder petrol engine. By the end of the War nearly 650,000 Jeeps had been produced.

Of the 800,000 plus 2$\frac{1}{2}$ ton capacity 6 x 6 trucks of the Second World War, GMC produced no less than 562,750 from 1939. Commonly known as the Jimmy (for GM) or Deuce and a Half (2$\frac{1}{2}$ ton) it was the most widely used tactical truck of the World War II. The GMC versions had six cylinder 104 bhp petrol engines and two range five-speed gearboxes. These light 6 x 6 trucks were made by many firms that had mass-production capabilities (Studebaker, International and GMC) and were the largest trucks that could be produced in such quantities.

In Britain, General Motors' Bedford factory produced over 250,000 trucks for the War effort. They were based on civilian models, though the 4 x 4 QL was quite a long way removed from these, apart from its six-cylinder 72 bhp petrol engine, being Bedford's first factory built forward control type. Bedford produced 52,245 QL models and these did much to replace the outdated 3 ton 6 x 4 types that had been the WD's principal preoccupation in the 1930s.

Opposite page top:
Most of France's production was decimated by the war or else fell into German hands. Before this happened, one of the more original designs appeared from Laffly in the mid 1930s. A 1940 example of the Laffly S25T is shown, it being a 6 x 6 with Laffly 60 CV 3.45 litre four-cylinder petrol engine. It had two paralled sets of prop shafts driving the wheels on each side and was partially built using Austro-Daimler patents. Similar machines were made by Hotchkiss which differed principally in the use of this famous old armament company's own engines. Some Lafflys also used Hotchkiss engines, or Peugeots in the lighter models.

Left and opposite page bottom:
The Spa CL39 was a product of the FIAT group produced between 1940 and 1945. It had a capacity of 1 tonne and was powered by a 25 bhp four-cylinder engine. The chassis view is of a 1938 Spa TL37, a normal control vehicle with 4 litre 52 bhp engine, four-wheel drive/steering and the unusual drive-shaft layout shown (similar to the experimental Holverta-Vulcan of 1926). The fifth shaft goes to the rear-mounted winch.

Britain had encouraged military vehicle standardisation throughout the empire in the 1930s and Canada, with its off-shoots of America's big three motor manufacturers, assumed the role of principal supplier (apart from Britain itself). General Motors and Ford had collaborated on Canadian Military Pattern (CMP) vehicles since 1936 and their vehicles, as a result, looked very similar. Here we see a Chevrolet with 1942 pattern CMP cab that has been rebodied after the war by Hands-England for oilfield work. It had an 85 bhp six-cylinder petrol engine and two range, five-speed gearbox. During the war years Canada produced slightly more than 865,000 military vehicles.

Below: There have been amphibious vehicles before and since, but few captured the public imagination, or were so widely seen, as the DUKW (the letters indicating D for 1942 when it was standardised, U for amphibious, K for all-wheel drive and W for tandem rear axles). GMC built 21,147 during the War, based on the "Jimmy" 2½ ton 6 x 6 truck with 'marinising' expertise from Sparkman and Stephens of New York, who were also involved with an amphibious version of the Ford Jeep. Some DUKWs are still employed in civilian roles today.

Opposite page top: The Morris-Commercial Quad gun tractor is one of a large number of preserved Second World War military vehicles in Britain. With the exception of a handful of Nash/Jeffery Quad and FWD Model Bs of the Great War and a few Latils of the inter-war period, very few pre 1940 off-road vehicles have survived. The Morris-Commercial had a 3.52 litre four-cylinder petrol engine developing 70 bhp, and a five-speed gearbox. Similar vehicles were built by Guy, the Canadian factories and others.

FWD of Cliftonville had survived the lean 'thirties principally by selling trucks to Public Utilities. For example, by 1940 no less than eight thousand snow ploughs were in use. As in the First World War, conflict brought an enormous increase in production and thirty thousand FWDs were built for the war effort. Amongst the most familiar was the SU-COE, a 5/6 tonner with six-cylinder petrol (Waukesha) or diesel (Cummins) engines and five-speed gearbox. The COE in the model designation stood for "cab over engine" or in other words, forward control.

Latil continued to be France's best known supplier of off-road vehicles. Here we have a TRPZ 120 bhp 6 x 6 recovery truck demonstrating its lifting capacity with a Latil 4 x 4 tractor. These tractors changed little in appearance from the 1920s to the 1970s and continued to have steering on all four wheels as well as separate driving and load carrying axles. Latil in 1955 joined the SAVIEM combine along with Renault and SOMUA, but in 1974 departed to continue making its 4 x 4 tractors under the name Brimont.

Scammell continued to be an important supplier of military vehicles during the Second World War. Amongst its many products were Pioneer tank recovery vehicles, and shown here is the early postwar development of this chassis, called the Explorer. It had 6 x 6 and utilised a Meadows 10.35 litre 175 bhp six-cylinder petrol engine. The amazing degree of axle articulation can be seen here, made possible by a transversely pivotted front axle with the rear wheels on the outer ends of walking beam transmission cases that were conventionally suspended via semi-elliptic springs attached at their mid-points to a single driven rear axle.

Oshkosh had a similar product range to FWD in the 1940s but was not so well known in the military field. It did however produce Hercules engined wreckers and snow clearance vehicles for runways as well as linesmen's and road building trucks. Shown dwarfing a late 1940s Austin car is a civilian 4 x 4 prime mover for use in the West Indian sugar cane plantations, where its ability to go into the fields and then deliver direct to the sugar mills greatly increased productivity.

Off Road

Right: It was not just load carriers and tractors that needed to operate off the metalled highway during the Second World War. Equally important were cranes to unload stores or ammunition and speed construction work. Into this latter category came high speed trenchers. The example depicted in this Museum of English Rural Life photograph is a Buckeye made in America but shown working in Warwickshire in 1943. Several other American firms made similar machines whilst off-road crane-carriers were produced by Dart, Hendrickson, Available, Coleman, Biederman, Brockway, Corbitt, FWD and others, plus firms that made both the crane and chassis themselves, like Lorain and Michigan.

Below: Several of the warring nations made half-tracked vehicles for maximum off-road traction and flotation. Germany was particularly wedded to the idea and produced trucks in many weight categories on tracks going right down to half-tracked motorcycles. Shown here is one of the lighter trucks, a 2 ton Opel Blitz Maultier (Mule). It had a 3.6 litre 68 bhp petrol engine, five-speed gearbox and driven front axle. Over five thousand Maultiers were produced by Ford, Magirus, Mercedes-Benz and Opel.

Opposite page bottom: As recounted earlier, the all-wheel driven AECs were closely-related to the original FWD Model B, as indeed was the FWD SU-COE. The famous 4 x 4 Matador accounted for almost ten thousand of the thirteen thousand military AECs made between 1939 and 1945. Rarer were the 0854 (diesel) and 854 (petrol) 6 x 6 versions which were most frequently encountered as 2,500 gallon aircraft refuellers for the RAF, which had 1,514 of them.

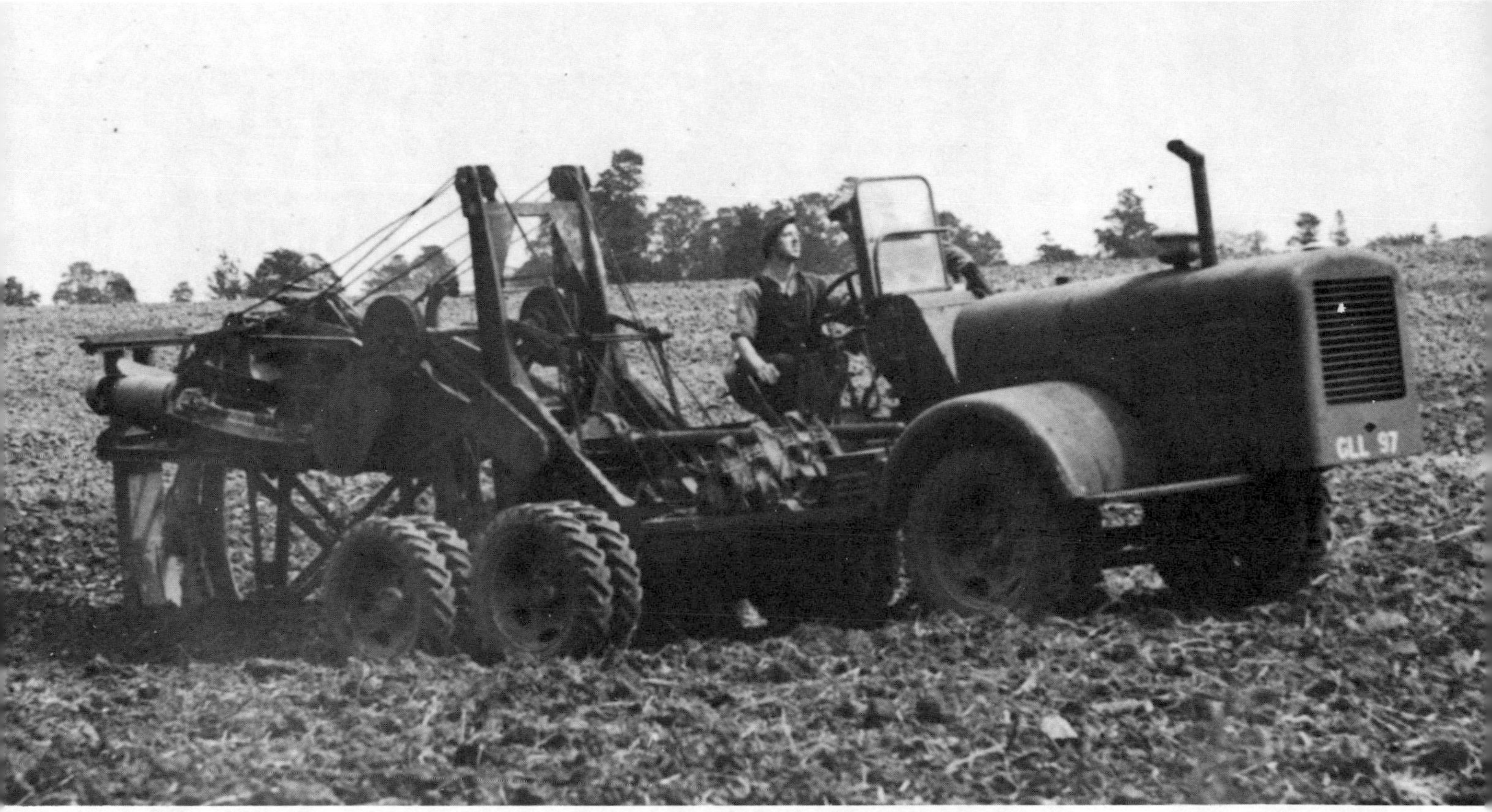
GLL 97

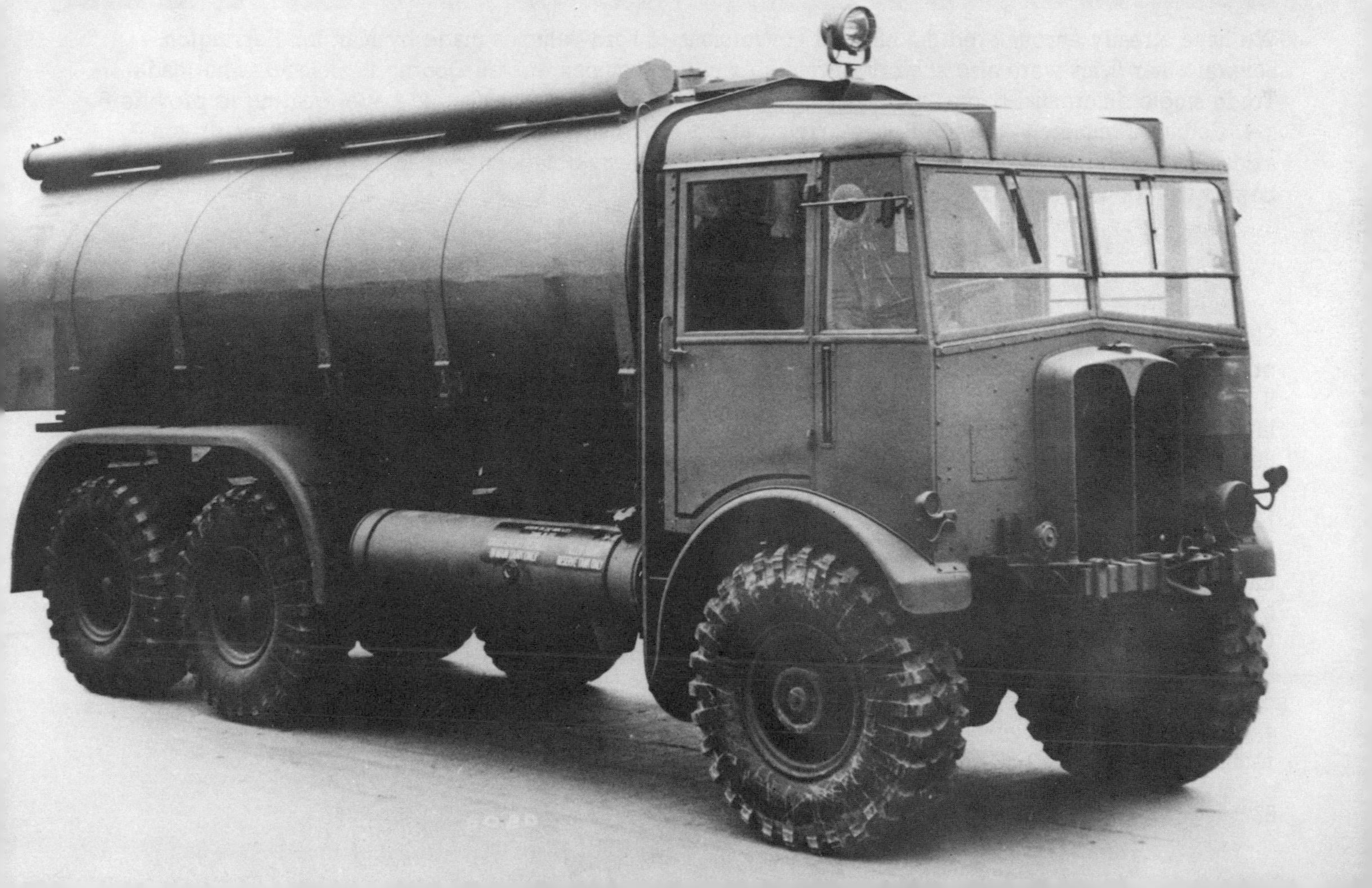

We have already encountered the off-road conversions of Ford vehicles made by Marmon-Herrington. Several other firms were also at work, including van der Trappen en van Doorne in Holland, who made Trado single differential bogies with walking beams containing drive shafts and bevel gearing to provide 6 x 4. County Commercial Cars in Britain arrived at 6 x 4 by more simple means, using two rear driven axles. This is their specification 36B field artillery tractor showing its military pattern trunnion mounted bogies with double springs.

Skoda of Czechoslovakia was primarily an armaments firm when it began to produce goods vehicles in 1925. These were British Sentinels made under licence or else products of the old established Laurin & Klement business which it had acquired. Off-road trucks followed in the 1930s and the firm became a major supplier to the German war machine of 4 x 4 and 6 x 6 vehicles, some of them the designs of Porsche. Here we see a 4 x 4 4S type load carrier reminiscent of an FWD SU-COE.

Countries like Switzerland and Sweden needed military vehicles to defend their neutrality. In Sweden the principal manufacturers then, as now, were Volvo and Scania. Shown is a Volvo armoured personnel carrier based on a TLV-141D 4 x 4 truck. It had a 5.65 litre 105 bhp overhead valve petrol engine and was in production from 1944. Note the chains on the tyres for extra grip and protection. The vehicle featured a power winch.

An interesting case of swords to ploughshares. The Dodge 1^1/$_2$ ton 6 x 6 was in production from 1942 and had a 92 bhp six-cylinder petrol engine and two range four-speed transmission. This one is shown at work in Pershore, Worcestershire in 1947 with a bale pickup developed by farmers W. O. Steele and Son, that was driven off the front-mounted winch. The 6 x 6 was closely related to the better known 4 x 4 Dodge "Beep" and was used for cargo and personnel transport.

Off Road

The O model Bedford was a militarised version of a standard civilian truck but with simplified sheet metal frontal treatment. It was a 4 x 2 vehicle in its military role, but as can be seen in this 1947 picture from the Museum of English Rural Life at Reading University, a cross-country version was envisaged by Opperman. It had a walking beam arrangement to give 6 x 4 via chains from the original axle and payload was $5\frac{1}{2}$ tons. Opperman was an English gear manufacturer whose production vehicle activities centred round the curious 1 x 3 Motorcart and an even stranger bubblecar. The fuel tank on the roof of the Bedford has, incidentally, been moved from its position on the side of the chassis occupied by one of the wheels.

From a British motor industry point of view, one of the most significant vehicles to follow the war was the Land-Rover and a very early prototype dating from 1947 is shown here. Rover was a car maker whose Government steel allocation was governed by its export success. Exports had not played much part in its past, so it decided to make an agricultural utility vehicle using Birmabright aluminium alloy bodywork. The first one was based on a Jeep with Rover engine and transmission, and had a central driving position like a tractor. Launched in 1948 using only Rover components, the Land-Rover became even better known than the Jeep in many parts of the world.

5 The 50s and 60s

During the 1950s and 1960s development of ever more sophisticated military vehicles took place. However, there were still thousands of ex-WD types with plenty of life left in them pouring onto the second-hand market. The period started with a major growth in the use of light 4 x 4 utilities of the Land-Rover type. Examples were built in Belgium, France, Italy, Germany and elsewhere. In the latter country the multi-purpose Unimog 4 x 4 had got off to a slow start in the late 1940s, but once adopted by Mercedes-Benz in 1951 its fortunes improved dramatically. The high cost of specialist vehicles led to several firms converting existing types for off-road use, examples shown in this chapter being Douglas, CCC and AWD.

In many undeveloped countries 4 x 4s were too sophisticated and expensive for many uses and several vehicles of the Farmobil type began to appear, though ultra cheap Japanese imports were beginning to have an impact.

Thanks to improving tyre technology it was possible to make vehicles which exerted almost as low ground pressure as crawlers. W.H. Albec's Rolligon tyres and Goodyear Terra-Tires were adopted on various vehicles, though Muskeg vehicles continued to run tracks over ordinary pneumatic tyres, and vehicles like the David and Amfirol tried other ingenious solutions to travel on wet marshland.

Perhaps most impressive of all in the 1950s and 1960s were the desert vehicles and dumptrucks which grew to colossal size without the constraints of road use. The dumptrucks are covered in greater detail in Nick Baldwin's book "Giant Dumptrucks" published by Haynes. The desert vehicles included the T600 Berliet, Atkinson Omega, Scammell Super Constructor, Thornycroft Mighty Antar and various Kenworths, many of which can be been in the following pages.

Commer Superpoise 4 x 4 conversion by AWD (see page 67). Note wider front axle requiring flared wings.

A 1964 30 cwt Bedford after conversion by AWD.

A newcomer in 1955 was All Wheel Drive of Camberley, England. Founded by A.J.F. Andrews, formerly with Gardner and Cheshire Engineering, it converted standard trucks for specialist roles. AECs became crane carriers, Commers, Bedfords and Leylands became 4 x 4s, but most importantly Ford Thames Traders were turned into 4 x 4, 6 x 4 and 6 x 6 lorries for many purposes. Cheshire post hole borers were fitted to many of them or else to purpose-built vehicles. These "Industrial Chassis" AWDs were assembled from proprietary components but were much more than mere conversions and came to include crane carriers and fire crash tenders. AWD assembled Michigan 4 x 4 loading shovels and in 1962 the two sides were divorced, with Andrews staying with Michigan and Vickers taking over the truck business, which became Vickers-AWD. It had moved to Bilston and in 1968 was transferred to South Marston, Swindon, where it ultimately concentrated on crane vehicles and was acquired by the George Cohen 600 Group, owners of Jones and other crane makers. Henceforth AWD was called Crane Travellers Ltd. and ceased to make general purpose off-road trucks. A small selection of its earlier products is shown on pages 66, 67, 68, 69.

Top:
A Jones crane on a waterproofed 6 x 6 AEC-based Industrial Chassis loads a similarly waterproofed Bedford RL 4 x 4.

Left:
An unusual version of a Thames Trader converted to 4 x 4 and used as a 34 seat bus in Laurenço Marques.

Off Road

Left:
4 x 4 kits were supplied by AWD to Ashok Leyland in India.

Below left:
A more familiar AWD conversion to a bonnetted Leyland Comet shown here on a Commercial Motor "road" test. The 4 x 4 in the background is a British Army Austin Champ.

Opposite page top:
Thames Traders came in all shapes and sizes after attention from AWD.

Below:
Several 6 x 4, 4 x 4 and 6 x 6 versions of the new 1964 Motor Panels cabbed Seddon range were produced.

Opposite page bottom right:
An S model Bedford converted to 6 x 6 to carry a Cheshire borer to inaccessible sites.

Off Road

The American equivalent of AWD/Crane Travellers was Crane Carrier Corp, which started in 1946 under the name of Zeligson as a chassis conversion specialist. The CCC name was adopted in 1953, when complete vehicles began to be built at Tulsa, Oklahoma. They included dumpers, concrete mixer, drilling and crane chassis, and log skidders. Shown is a "Rough Duty" 6 x 6 diesel powered chassis of about 1960 with planetary reduction axles and Chicago cab usually seen on International Harvester trucks. International also made heavy duty off-road models at the time and added their Jeep-like Scout 4 x 4 in 1961.

Right and bottom left and right:
Very low ground pressure was exerted by vehicles with Terra-Tires or, in this case, Rolligon Airbags. The Rolligon 6660 ten ton capacity 6 x 6 of the late 1960s was amphibious, could climb a sixty per cent gradient and achieve 20 mph. It had a 120 bhp six-cylinder diesel and four-speed transmission. Steering was by hydraulic centre pivot. In water it was limited to 2 mph and 6000 lbs load in addition to its 10,500 lbs unladen weight. The Rolligon Corporation was based at the time in Houston and Stafford, Texas, USA.

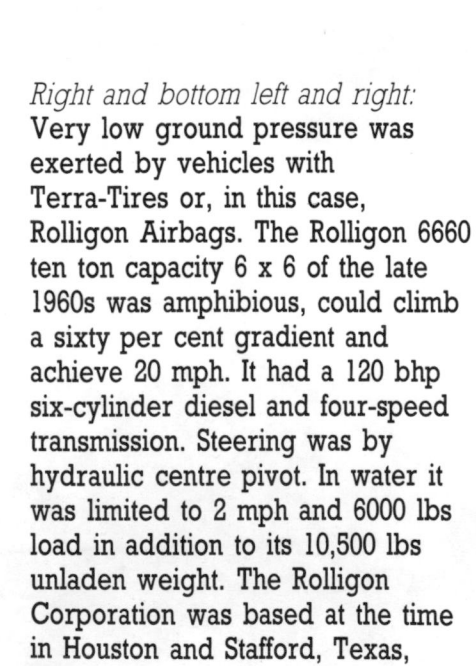

In 1961/2 this Büssing Burglöwe LS55 Allrad (the latter word signifying all-wheel drive) covered 30,000 kilometres on the Austrian Guinea expedition and twice crossed the Sahara desert. It had a 110 bhp 5.43 litre six-cylinder diesel and had a GVW of 10.2 tonnes (6.15 tonnes payload). In 1962 the German Büssing company took over a Borgward plant that made 4 x 4 trucks and continued to produce these for the German army until 1968. From 1969 it developed close links with MAN and was fully absorbed by this firm two years later.

Right and below:
Duplex had been making 4 x 4 trucks in Michigan since 1909. In 1955 it was acquired by crane maker Warner and Swasey, best known for its Gradall (chassis which were made for the British market by AWD). Shown here is a 1958 4 x 4 snow plough in use by the US Corps of Engineers for runway clearance and a view in their factory at the time showing 4 x 4 highway maintenance vehicles and a 6 x 6 half-cab crane carrier.

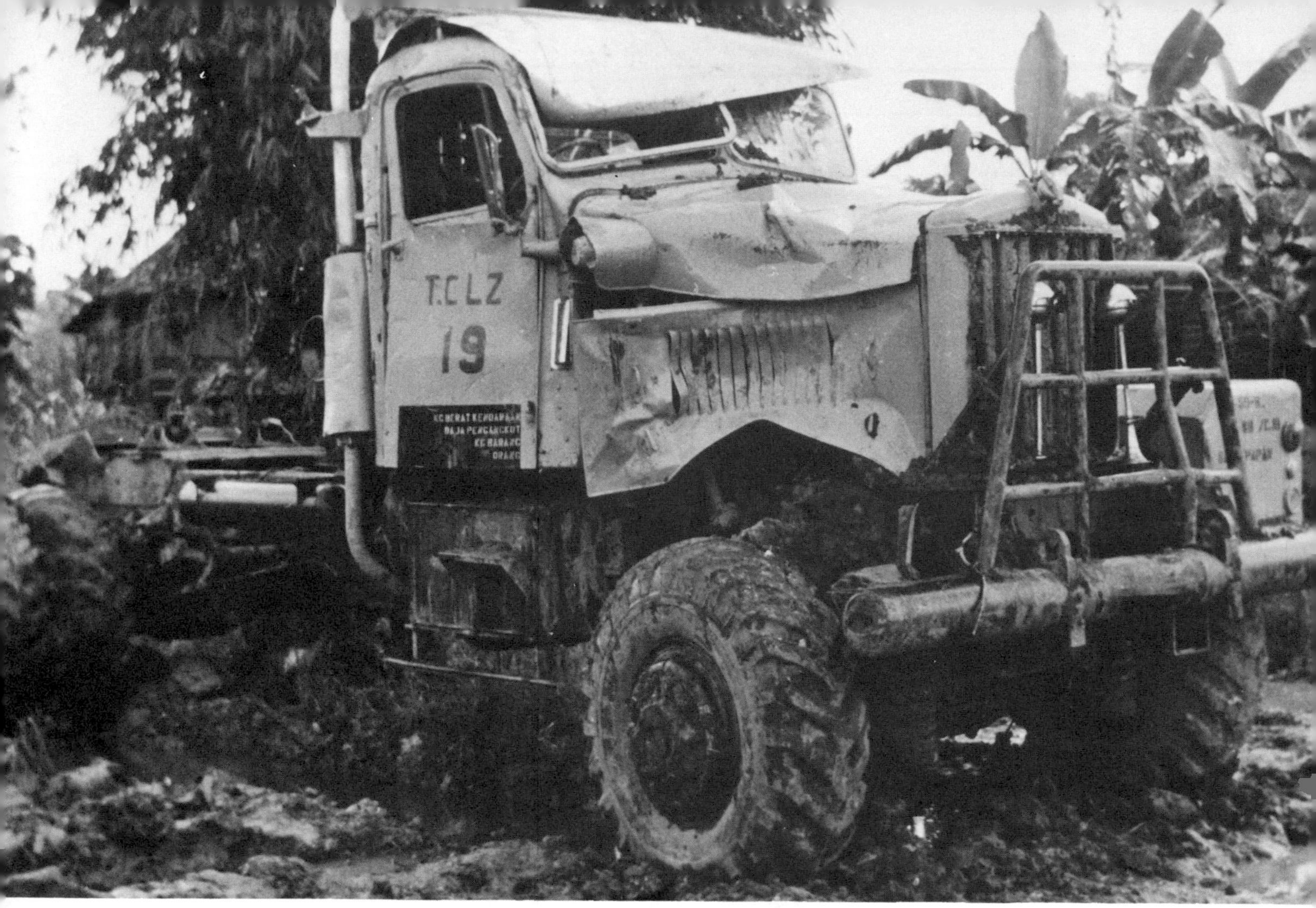
T.C LZ
19

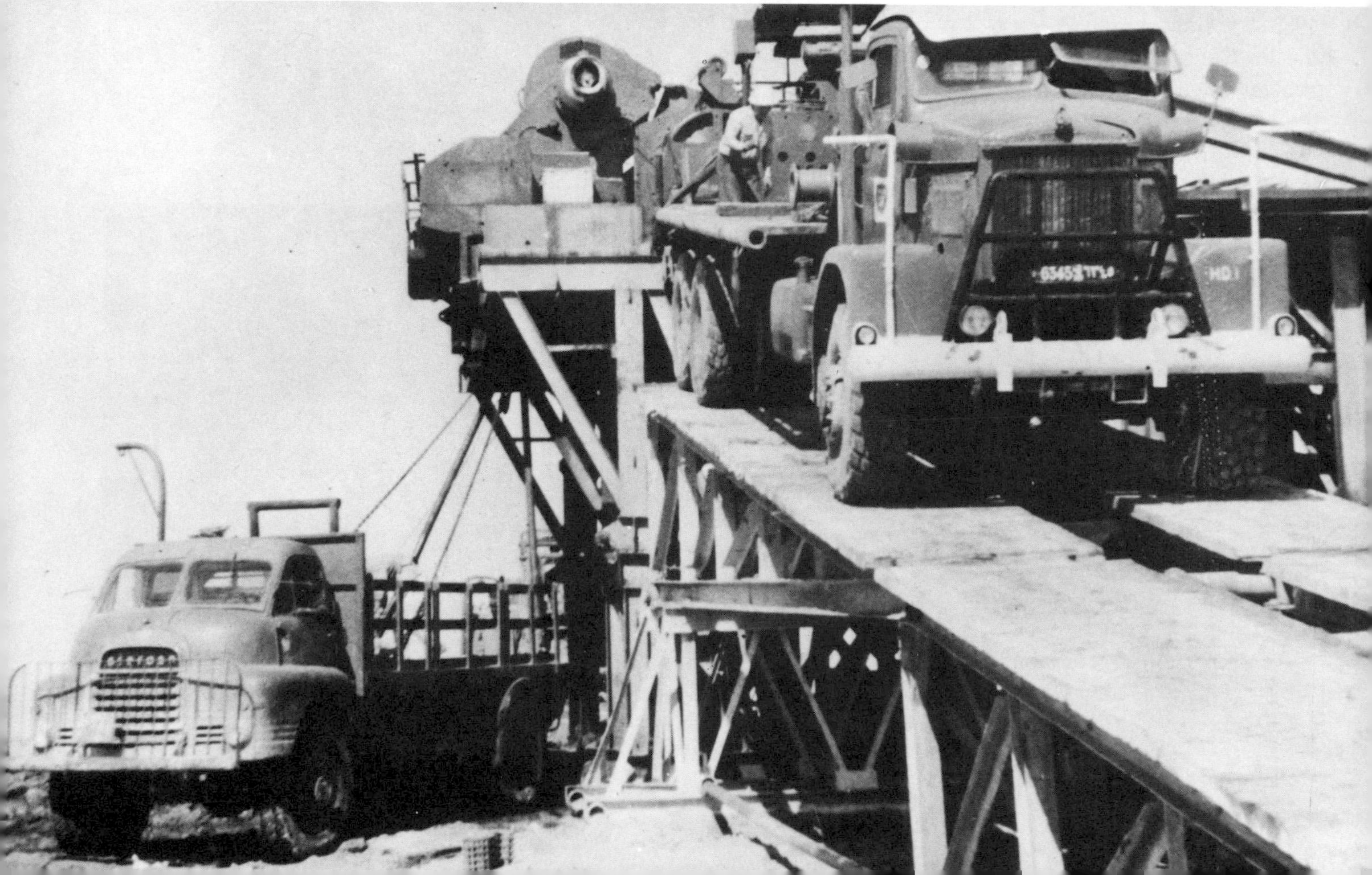

All four photographs: Scammell's off-road vehicle activities were by no means diminished by the Leyland takeover of 1955. Here we have a 4 x 4 Mountaineer still ready for work in Indonesia despite having turned over, a Super Constructor unloading oilfield equipment alongside a Bedford RL with gin poles, a Constructor on a Middle Eastern beach with the inevitable Land-Rovers and a group consisting of a Mack, a Constructor and a Thornycroft crane carrier.

Off Road

Opposite page top:
This 1968 photograph depicts a prototype 6 x 6 vehicle made by United States Steel as a military $2^1/_2$ ton go-anywhere (5 tons on road) load carrier. The USS XM761 was capable of over 50 mph and had a 145 bhp multi-fuel engine with five-speed manual or six-speed automatic gearbox. Rear suspension was independent by coil springs and swing arms. An unusual feature was the brake drums on the outside of the wheels. The XM761 was intended as a contender for the US Army $2^1/_2$ ton truck order typically filled by normal control M series vehicles from Reo, Studebaker, Kaiser, Jeep, etc.

Rugged tracks for the Canadian logging industry were built by Pacific of North Vancouver from 1947. Later they added oilfield and other off-road vehicles and were for a time a subsidiary of International Harvester. In the 1980s Pacific instead became part of the British Inchcape Group. Shown is a 6 x 4 truck with semi-trailer at work in British Columbia. The type was available with Cummins, Caterpillar or Detroit diesels of up to 500 bhp and had water-cooled brakes for long descents to the nearest river or sawmill.

Opposite page bottom:
The Albion-Cuthbertson Water Buffalo was an ingenious vehicle designed by Cuthbertson and built by Albion of Scotstoun, Glasgow, a member of the Leyland Group since 1951. It was a low-flotation tractor and load carrier intended to tame the peat bogs of Scotland. A 1959 version able to float is shown towing a ten ton 'slipe', though a twenty-eight ton trailer with ten tyres was also available.

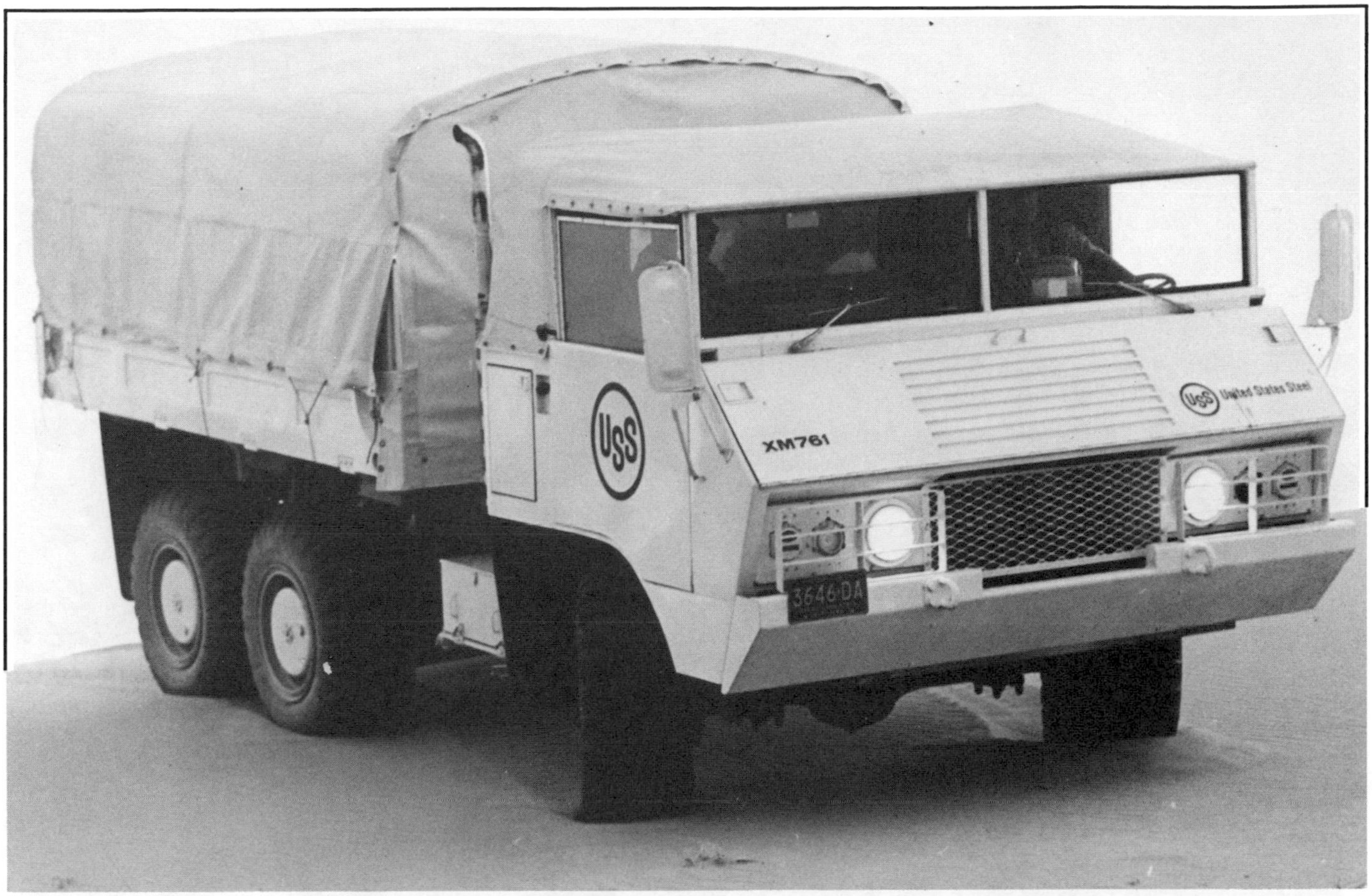
USS
XM761
USS United States Steel
3646 DA

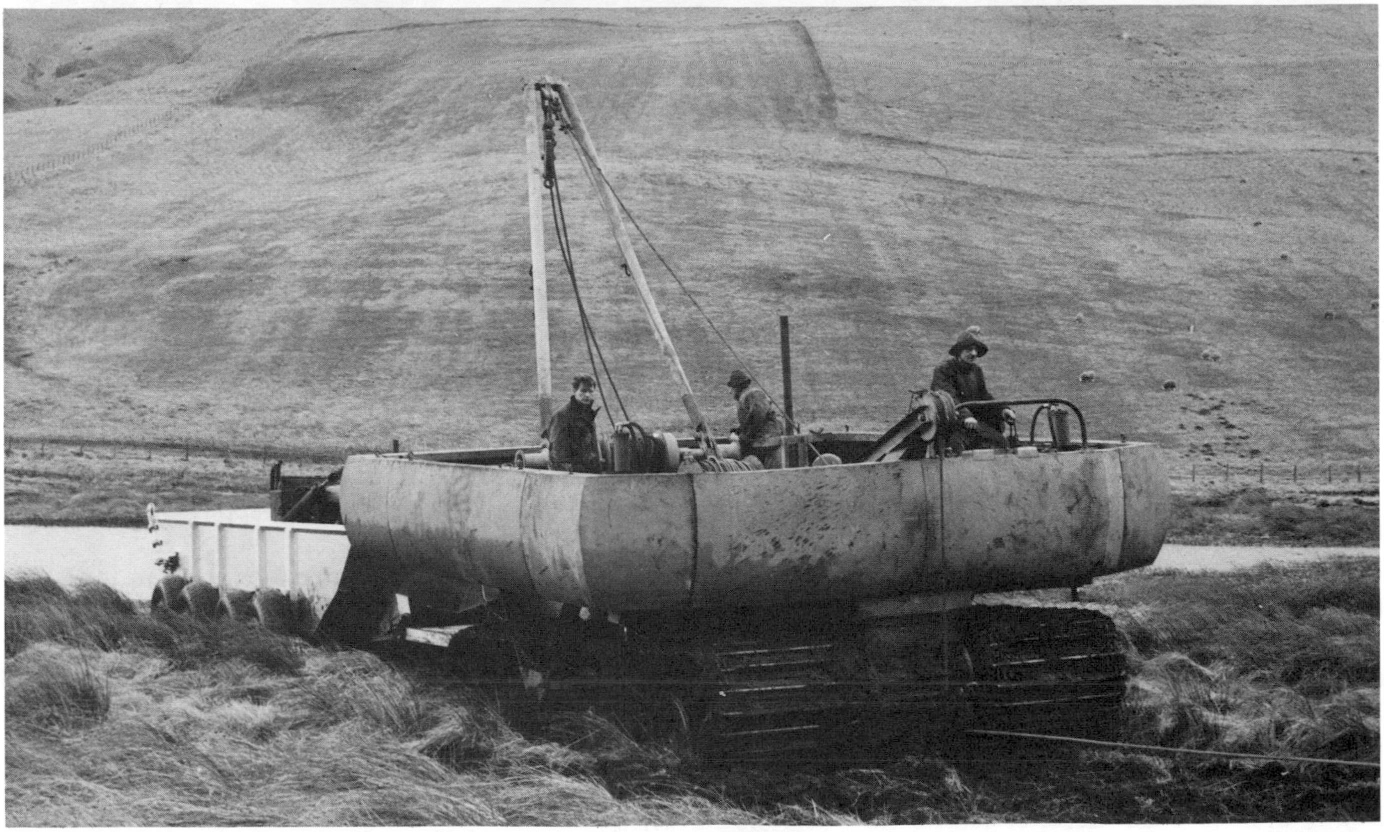

Above: Oshkosh made quite a speciality of concrete placement vehicles and in 1955 introduced a 50-50 series in which weight distribution was equalised by setting the front axle well back from the engine. Versions were ultimately offered with up to six axles. In 1975 Oshkosh introduced a forward placement mixer chassis in which the drum was turned round and discharged over the one man cab at the front. The engine pod was at the rear.

Opposite page top: Scammell and Kenworth shared most of the heavy oilfield truck market in the 1950s and the British firm of Atkinson was keen to break into it. The Omega was a 6 x 6 design that appeared in 1957 with 275 bhp Rolls-Royce diesel. Of the few that were built some had Cummins 335 bhp diesels. The example shown here was on test in the Egyptian desert in 1958. Note the all-conquering Kenworth in the background.

Opposite page bottom: The Michigan division of Ling-Temco-Vought produced the 6 x 6 Gama Goat in the early 1960s for civilian customers. They were supplied for US military evaluation in 1965 and entered series production with the Condec Corporation from 1969. The rear portion pivoted but the front and rear axles steered. Engines originally available included air-cooled Chevrolet Corvair six-cylinder gasolene and Detroit three-cylinder diesel of 80 bhp and 103 bhp respectively.

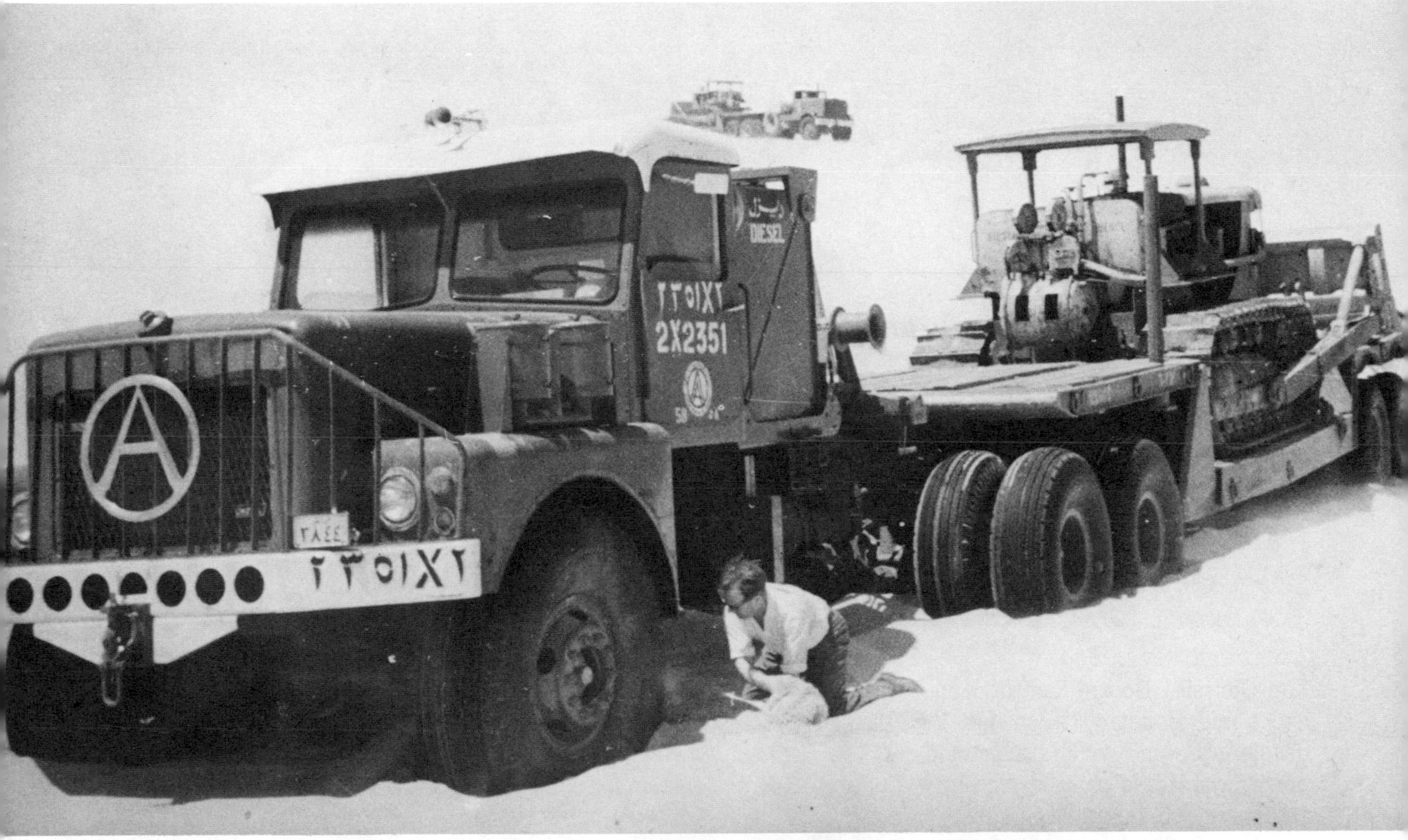
DIESEL
2X2351

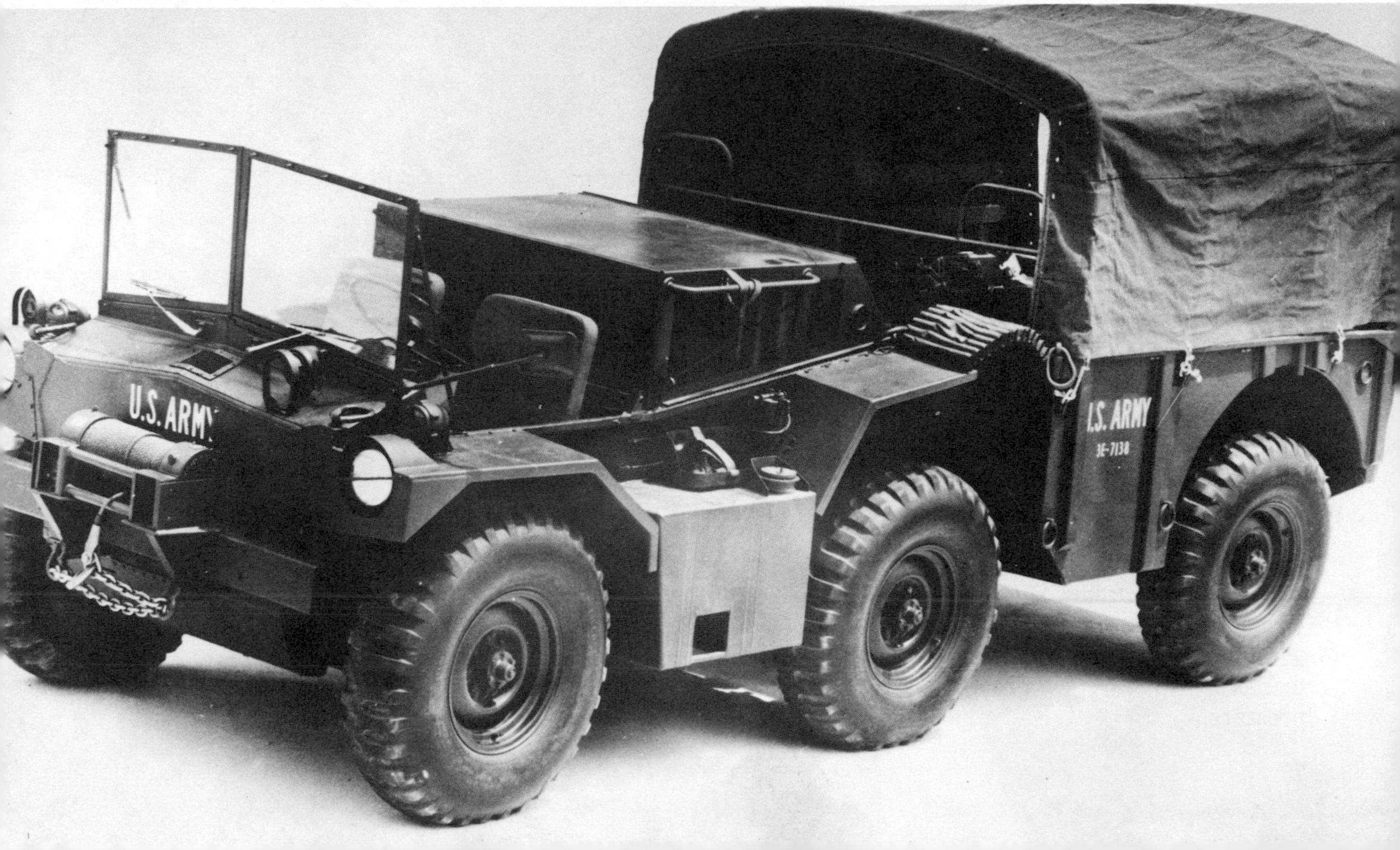
U.S. ARMY
U.S. ARMY
3E-7138

Above left and right:
The Chrysler Dodge Ram of 1966 had a mid-mounted 318 cu. ins. V8 gasolene engine which transmitted power via Morse chain drive and automatic two range three-speed gearbox to the driven front and rear axles. The Ram was air-transportable, amphibious and had independent suspension at front and rear as well as disc brakes and power steering. It was able to transport 1¼ ton loads to virtually any destination.

Right and opposite page top:
Fully tracked vehicles for traversing Canadian muskeg are made by several firms. Shown is a Nodwell carrying pipes (note the pneumatic tyred wheels inside the tracks, Nodwell having built such vehicles since 1953). The other vehicles are a Foremost stake truck and a convoy of Bombardiers carrying cable drums. Foremost, which now owns Nodwell, additionally made wheeled versions that also exert very low ground pressure.

Off Road

Following six photographs:
As well as AWD there was another newcomer to the British off-road scene. This was Douglas of Cheltenham, which since 1966 has made mostly dock and airport tugs. However, from 1947 to that date it made a wide assortment of custom chassis and all-wheel drive versions of standard trucks. Shown are a small selection, including McAlpine concrete skip on a 1959 Meadows 85 bhp engined DM4 Transporter, bonnetted 6 x 6 TK6 18 tonner (35 tons with semi-trailer) shown on 228 DG trade plates and Commer two-stroke diesel 4 x 4 on sand tyres used for spraying the Tunisian desert with an oil by-product prior to planting. Then there is a 196 bhp Rolls-Royce petrol engined 6 x 6 Firefly crash tender of 1958, a Pathfinder 4 x 4 with independent front suspension, Commer cab and Rootes 85 bhp petrol engine and finally an early Commer Superpoise based 6 x 4 with "headache rack".

PINE

4X4
DOUGLAS

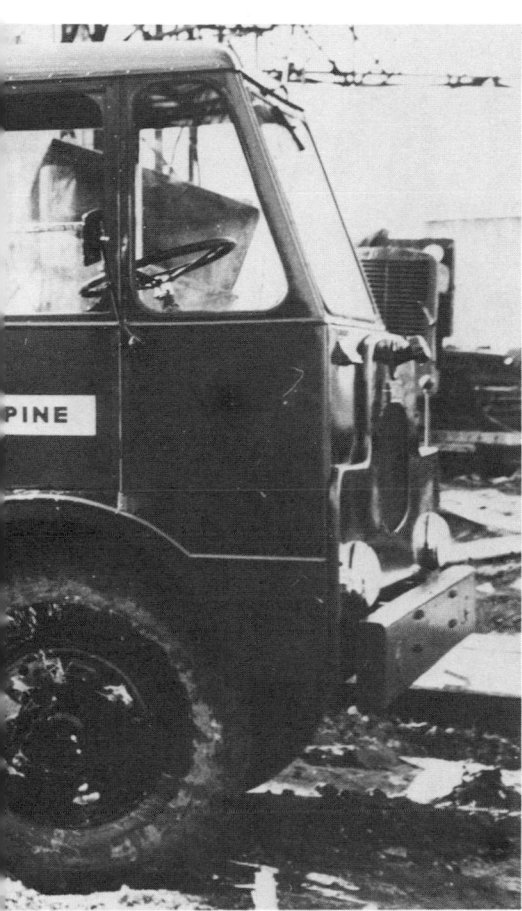

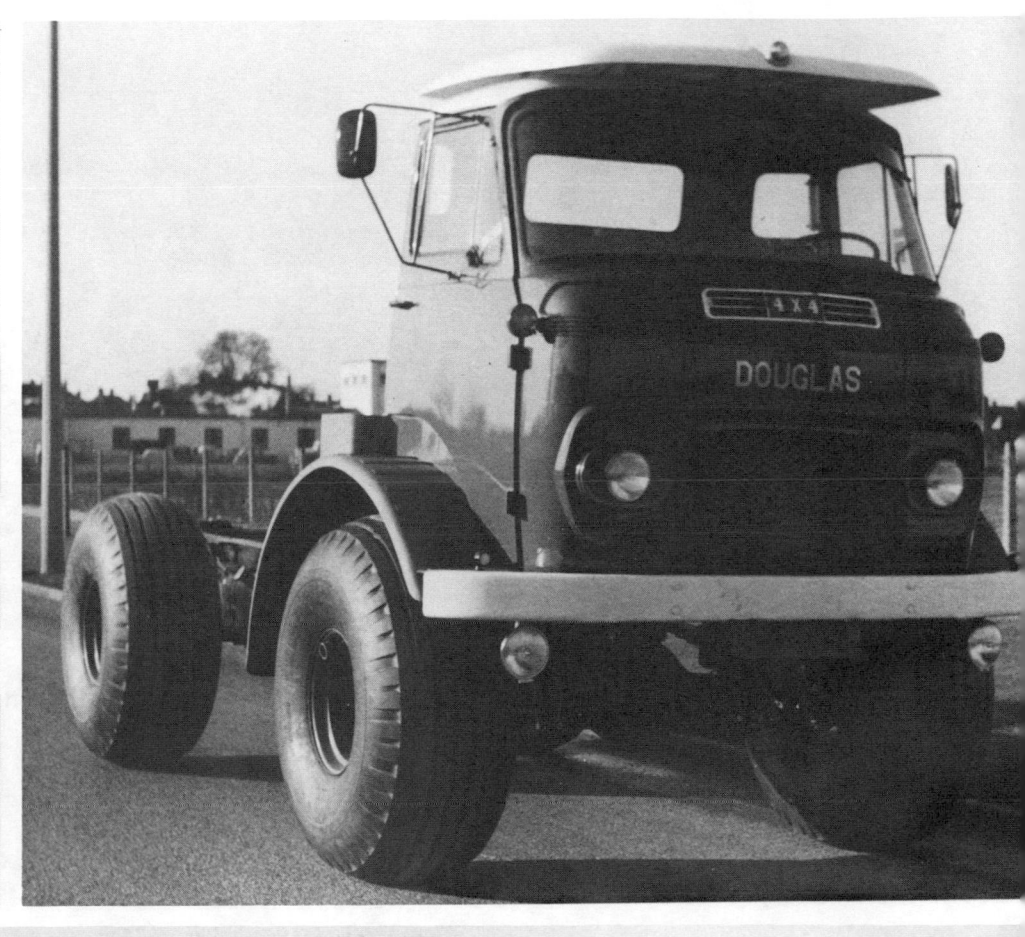

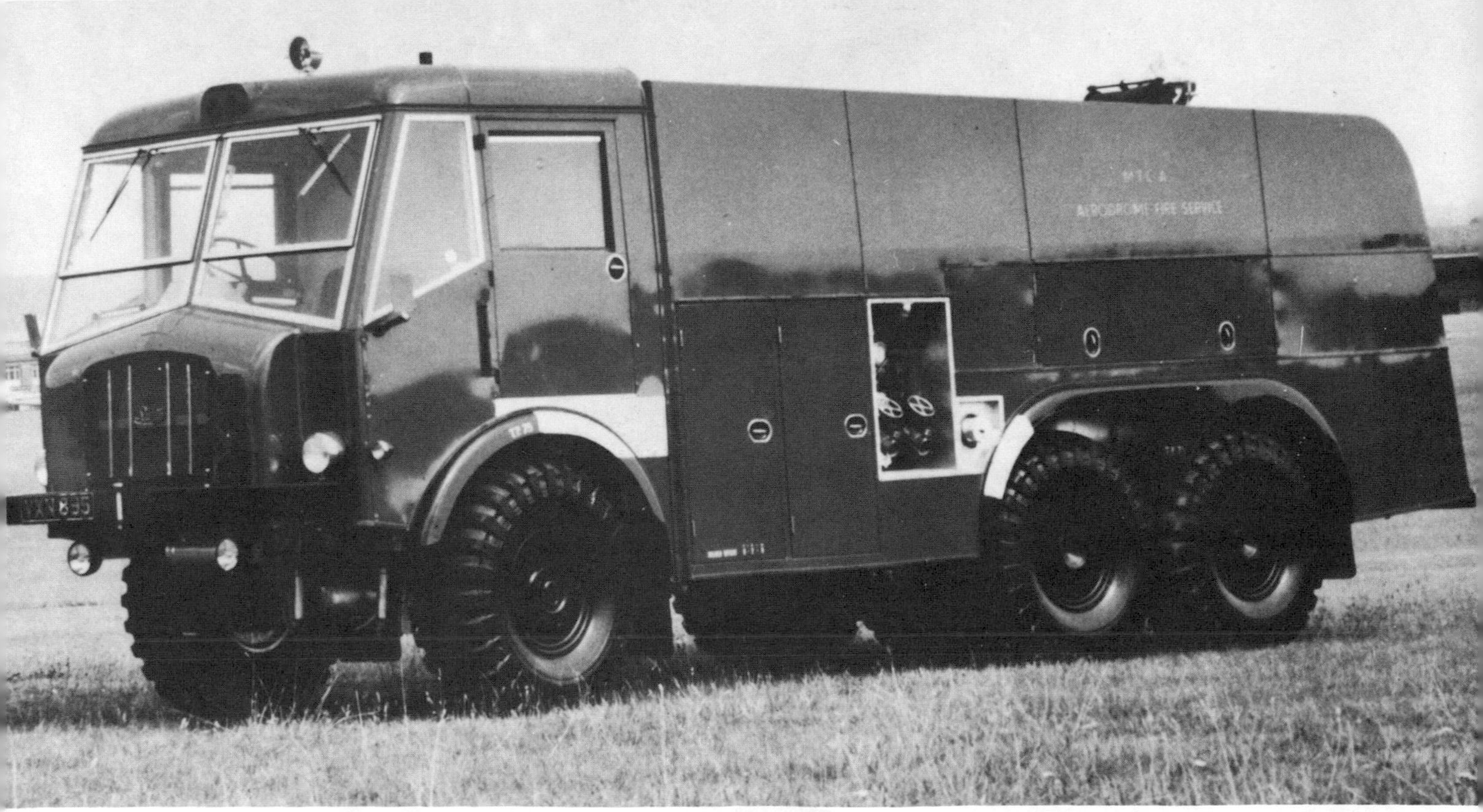
M.T.C.A.
AERODROME FIRE SERVICE

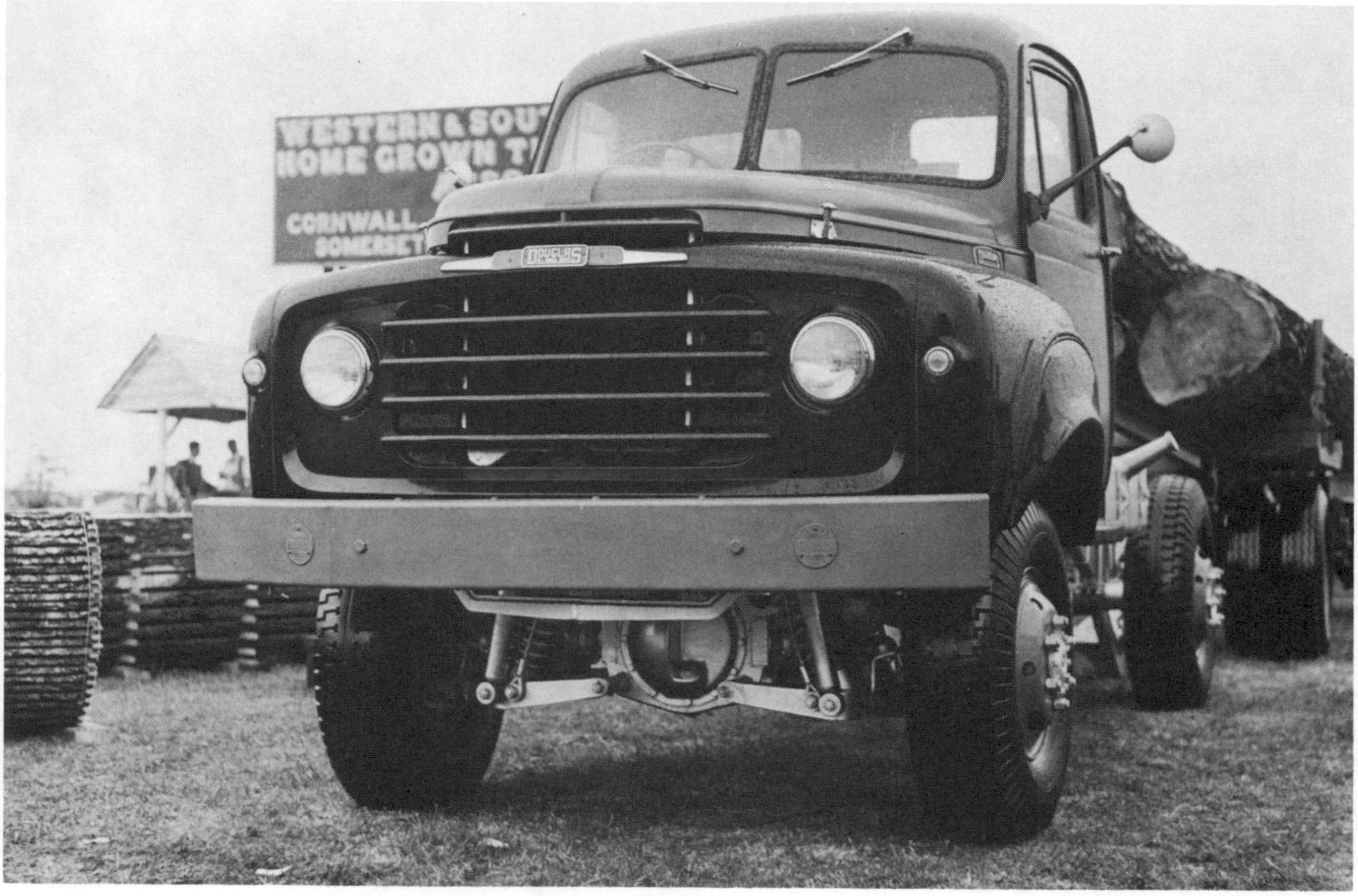
DOUGLAS
CORNWALL
SOMERSET

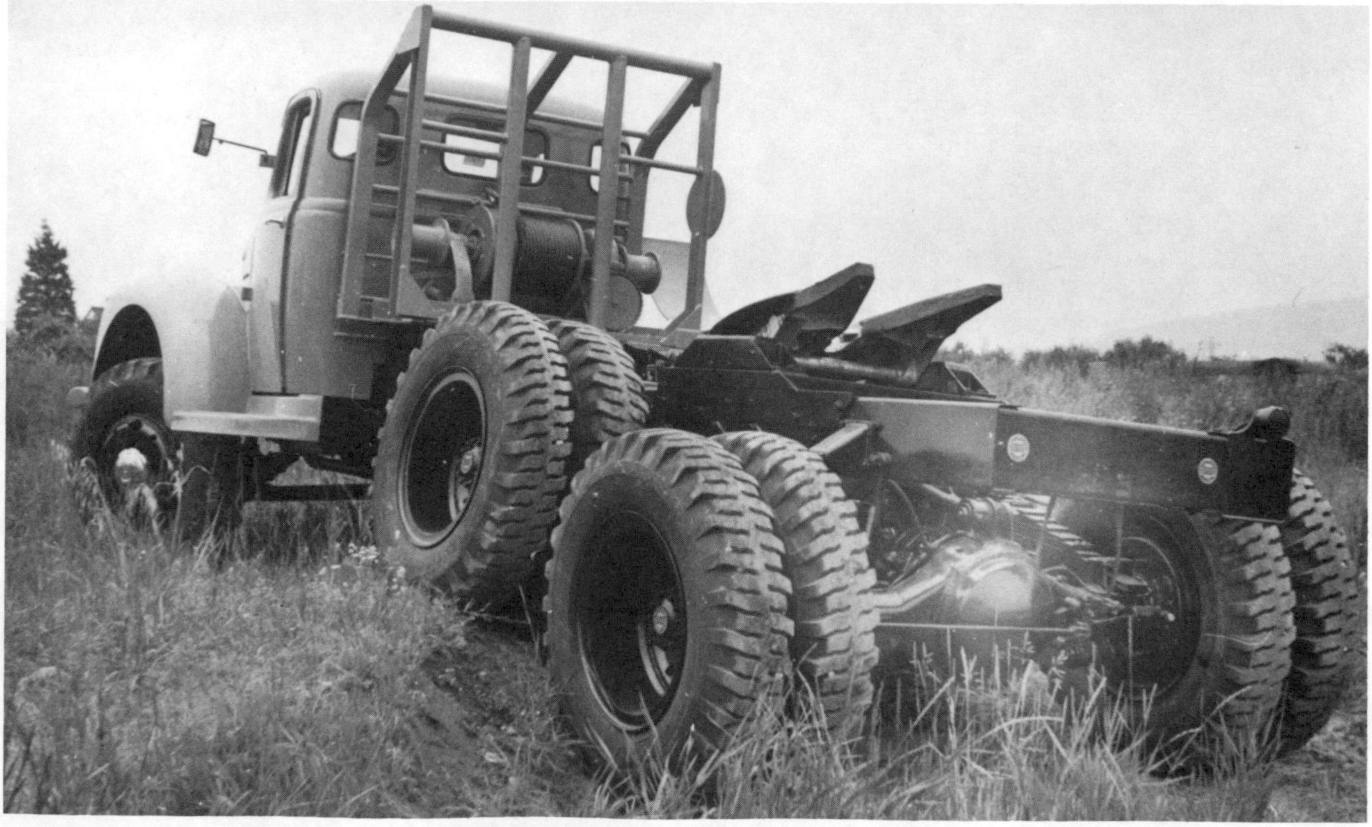

Amongst the factory built mass-produced 4 x 4 trucks of the 1950s, as opposed to specialist conversions, was the one ton Austin K9 and the even better known Bedford 3-4 ton RL. This 1954 Austin was rated for 1½ tons in civilian guise and had a 90 bhp six-cylinder petrol engine and two range four-speed gearbox. The same firm's Champ appeared in the background earlier, this being a Rolls-Royce or Austin A90 powered ¼ ton 4 x 4 originally developed by Nuffield (Morris).

The little Pony of 1962 onwards was built by the Dutch firm DAF incorporating its Variomatic infinitely variable belt transmission. The Pony was air-portable and could be driven as shown, or else from the rear, by an infantryman on foot. Power came from a 600 cc two cylinder air-cooled petrol engine as used in the Daffodil car.

The Alvis Stalwart was the 6 x 6 amphibious member of the FV600 military range introduced in 1952 that also included the Salamander fire engine, Saladin armoured car and Saracen armoured personnel carrier. The Stalwart had three equally spaced wheels on each side, of which all but the rear steered. Power was provided by an eight-cylinder Rolls-Royce petrol or multi fuel engine. There was independent suspension and disc brakes on all wheels and load capacity was five tons. Alvis of Coventry still produces military vehicles, though nowadays with tracks.

The 4 x 4 Unimog started life in 1948 as a Universal Motor Gerat (Universal Motor Unit) and was taken over by Daimler-Benz in 1951, who transferred production from Goppingen to Gaggenau and continued to use Mercedes-Benz petrol and diesel engines of various sizes. Over the years the Unimog has been adapted for many different duties. The version shown here has a 6 x 6 conversion by Lesa of Schevenhutte who called it their LUF 111A model. It had a 100 bhp six-cylinder engine and payload including bodywork was 6.6 tonnes.

The David Buggy entered production at Ardco of Houston, Texas, in the mid 1950s. It was a simple amphibious vehicle with air-cooled engine, six forward speeds (26 mph maximum), built-in winch and rubber or aluminium "tyres". A twin engined version was available from 1959 as were various pieces of amphibious equipment for it to tow. The Buggy was particularly suited to operation in the swampy Louisiana/Gulf coast region.

The Thornycroft Big Ben came in forward and normal control form in the 1950s and early 1960s. The normal control type had 6 x 4 or 6 x 6 and in general appearance was similar to the larger Antar (which had first appeared in 1949 with an 18 litre Rover engine) and export versions of the smaller 6 x 4 Trusty. Thornycroft also produced a 6 x 6 Nubian for oilfield and crash tender duties. Thornycroft was acquired by AEC in 1961 and all its models with the exception of the Nubian and LD55 were discontinued by the time that production was transferred to Scammell in 1969.

Since the Jeep, Land-Rover and Unimog came on the scene in the 1940s there have been numerous similar vehicles produced all over the world. It is impossible to show them here, expecially as many have been covered in Haynes Olyslager's "Cross-Country Cars from 1945" and Shire Publication's "Land-Rover and Four Wheel Drive". As an example of one of the less familiar newcomers we show here a 1969 Russian UAZ for 0.8 tonne loads. It had a 2445 cc four-cylinder 80 bhp petrol engine.

An idea that had been tried on cars and tractors in the 1920s was revived in Holland by Amfirol after the Second World War. It consisted of a vehicle propelled by twin screws that also provided flotation. It could carry 2.5 tonnes when floating and achieve up to 30 km/h. The screws allowed it to travel forwards or sideways and could also be moved out of parallel for turning round in its own length. Transmission was by the DAF Variomatic system, and the Amfirol was built of stainless and manganese steel.

The famous Belgian armaments and motorcycle firm of FN also made cars and commercials. The latter were made until 1963, and thereafter FN built only to specific military orders. The 1¹/₂ tonne Ardennes 4 x 4 model shown dates from 1957 and had a 4.7 litre petrol engine and eight-speed transmission. Numerous other European firms made 4 x 4 trucks in this weight range at the time, those for military use being illustrated in the Olyslager/Haynes book "Military Vehicles from 1945".

Large dumptrucks often work in hard surfaced quarries and do not require all-wheel drive. However, for variable construction sites and rough haul roads some firms provided 4 x 4 on their machines. Examples were International Payhauler, Faun, Oshkosh and the Krupps shown here. These are AMK18 models for 18 tonne loads with Krupp 220 bhp two stroke diesels. The German Krupp firm had made dumptrucks since 1951 and still produces truck-mounted cranes today, though regular truck production ended in 1968.

Above: The French firm of Hotchkiss founded at the time of the Franco-Prussian War by the American Benjamin B. Hotchkiss, the originator of the machine gun, made Jeeps under licence from 1953 to 1970. It also made larger 4 x 4 trucks like this PL 90 three tonner of 1967. Another well known French car and truck maker to produce Jeep-type vehicles was Delahaye from 1949 whilst Minerva, a car firm of similar background in Belgium, made Land-Rovers under licence before developing its own 4 x 4s in 1954.

Opposite page top: Light and simple cross country vehicles could get by with just rear-wheel drive if they were small enough to be manhandled out of difficulty. The Kraka power cart made in Germany was also produced as the Diana shown here by the MV motorcycle firm in Italy in the mid 1960s. The engine was at the rear and there were six seats. A similar but even simpler device was the Greek-built Chrysler Farmobil intended as a multi-purpose vehicle for impoverished rural area.

Opposite page bottom: FIAT continued to be Italy's principal producer of off-road vehicles and in the 1960s it even produced a version of the M type 6 x 6 US military pattern vehicle using its own 220 bhp engine under the designation FIAT-OM 6600. Meanwhile, Alfa-Romeo was still a rival and produced a light 4 x 4 called the Matta in 1951, of which around two thousand were built. Shown is a contemporary heavier 4 x 4, the Alfa-Romeo 450 CIL Militare, for 3.5 tonne loads.

Off Road

The British firm Unipower had a rather similar background to Latil, having produced 4 x 4 logging vehicles since the late 1930s. Before that and again after the War it had made 6 x 4 versions of existing 4 x 2 trucks. In 1968 it made a Perkins V8 powered Invader chassis suitable for various off-road duties and one is shown here before receiving cab and bodywork. It was not a sales success against cheaper ex-WD types, but the firm continues to make high powered airfield fire crash tenders.

France had commercial and political interests in the Sahara and various vehicles were built over the years to tap its oil wealth. One of the most spectacular was the 1957 Berliet T100 6 x 6 made in forward and normal control forms. Shown is a V12 30 litre, 600 bhp Cummins engined giant being inspected by soldiers in the desert. The truck could gross one hundred tonnes. Willème was another French company to produce mammoth oilfield and construction industry trucks at the time.

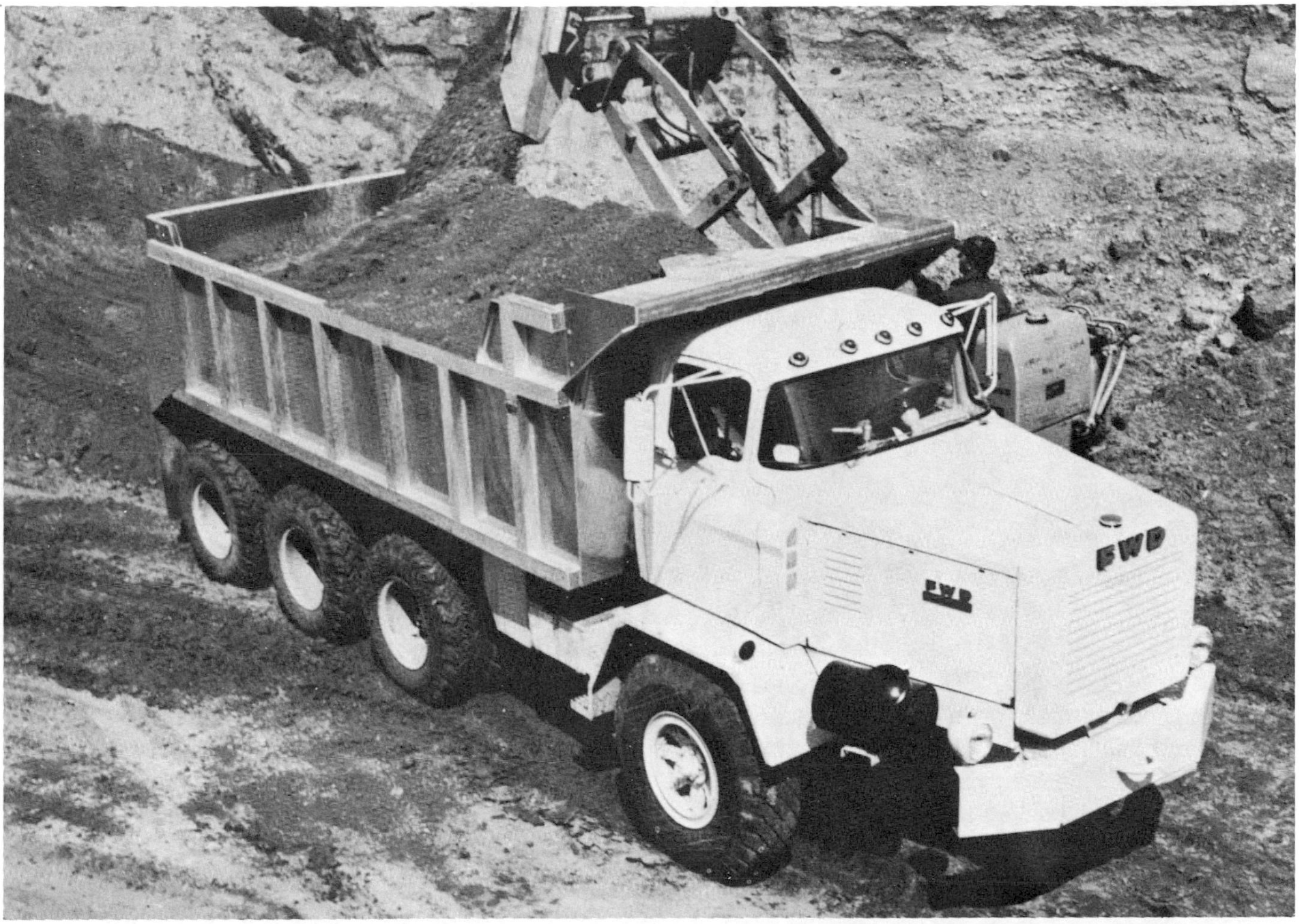
FWD
FWD

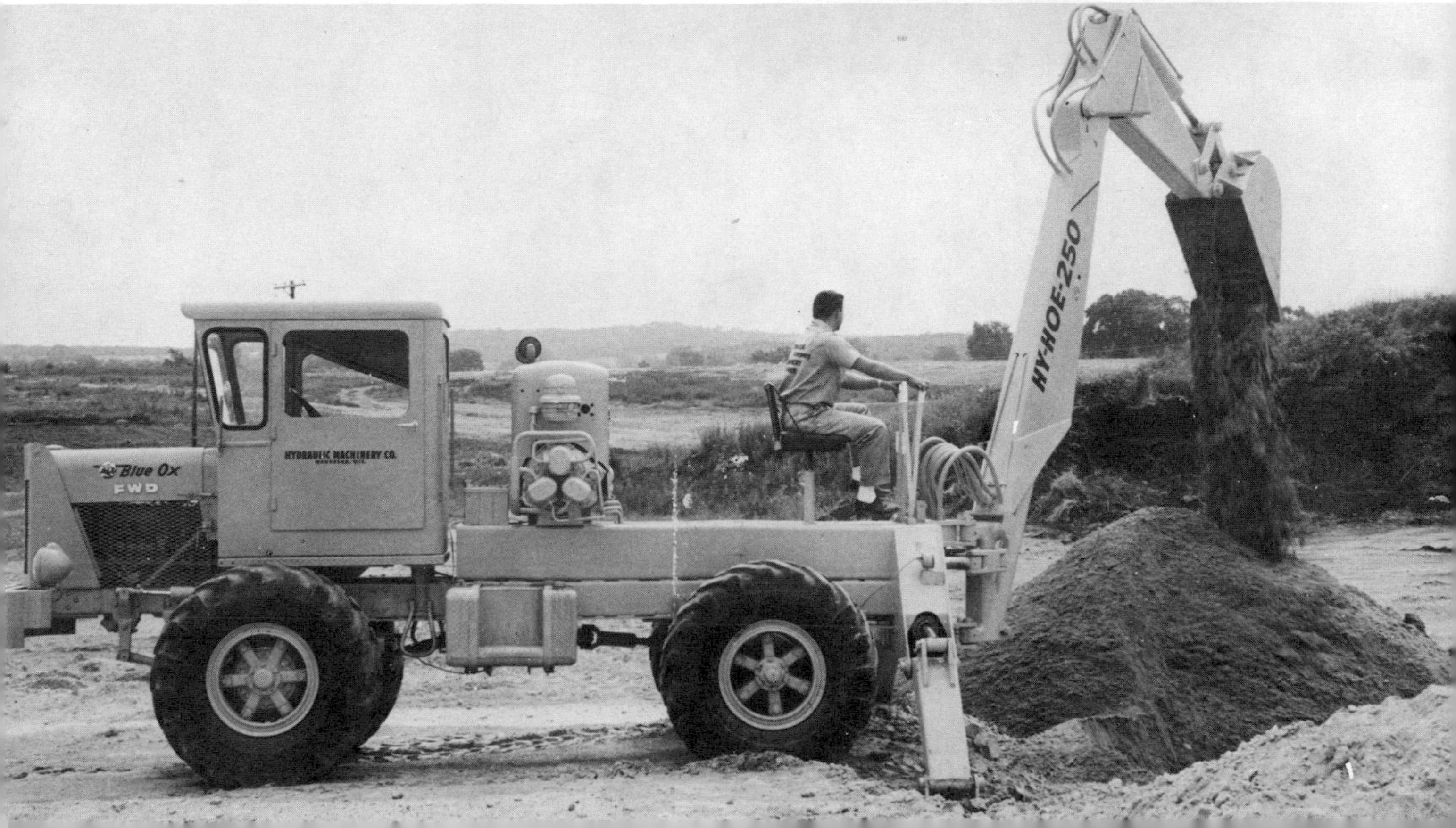
Blue Ox
FWD
HYDRAULIC MACHINERY CO.
HY-HOE-250

This and previous page: **FWD** continued to make one of the widest assortments of off-road vehicles in America. Amongst them were concrete placers, utility trucks, fire appliances, haulage models, crane carriers and military types. By way of example we show here a four-axle conventional tipper with set-back steering axle, a Blue Ox carrying a Hy-Hoe excavator, a view of the crane carriers and other vehicles in the factory park in 1958 and an 8 x 8 Teracruzer also of 1958. The latter had 42 inch wide Goodyear Terra-Tires and a Continental Packett opposed eight-cylinder air-cooled 250 bhp engine with Allison semi-automatic transmission. Payload was 17,000 lbs and the Teracruzer carried Matador guided missiles.

The Polish Star factory was the country's first producer of heavy trucks after the Second World War. It introduced its 66 model in 1958 as a military 6 x 6 with 105 bhp six-cylinder petrol engine and five-speed two range gearbox. Cross-country payload was $2\frac{1}{2}$ tons or 4 tons on hard surfaces. A broadly similar vehicle is still in production with a much modernised French Chausson designed cab.

County Commercial Cars of Fleet, Hampshire, UK, became best known for 4 x 4 farm tractors in this period, but also made an ingenious forward control load carrier or tractor based on Ford components. A 1968 version of its FC 654 is shown hauling a King ten ton capacity trailer. The County had a 65 bhp Ford diesel. A 4 x 4 version of the Ford Transit was available from County in the 1980s.

This Russian monster is a 1965 Yermak. It had a double glazed, air conditioned cab for operating in extreme temperatures. Tyre pressure on the six driven wheels could be adjusted from the cab whilst travelling. The Yermak could carry twenty-five ton loads and was powered by a 320 bhp diesel.

We'll leave the last words in this Chapter to two formidable off-roaders – Scammell and Caterpillar. Here the winch on the crawler is being used to hoist tree trunks (via a pulley high up a giant tree) onto the semi-trailer attached to a 4 x 4 Mountaineer.

6 Jeeps, Japs and Giants

Amazingly enough there are still plenty of 45 year old war veterans still giving good service as loggers and wreckers. However, the real development of note in the 1970s and 1980s has been the massive inroads that Japanese vehicles have made in markets traditionally catered for by America and Europe. Many of these 4 x 4s are lighter leisure vehicles by Daihatsu, Suzuki, Isuzu, Toyota, Nissan and Subaru, but higher up the weight range Japan and other Far Eastern manufacturers have made steady inroads. Against this background the Land-Rover had to be completely redesigned in the 1980s to come more into line with Range-Rover standards of ride and refinement. Mercedes has also entered the leisure field, leaving the Unimog to its industrial and agricultural duties. America too saw many new rivals to the famous Jeep, that itself had become far more refined over the years.

Ever since the 1950s there had been a demand for increasingly large off-road dump trucks. The principal development amongst quarry and construction vehicles in the last two decades has been the revival of the pivot-steer idea used by Pavesi sixty years before. In the up to fifty ton dump market pivot-steer types have largely ousted traditional trucks and come with 4 x 4, 6 x 4 or 6 x 6.

In this final chapter we also examine the growth of several important newcomers like MOL in Belgium, Brimont the successor to Latil in France, DJB in Britain, Foremost in Canada and RFW in Australia. Space prevents a detailed look at the activities of the famous existing makers like Scammell and FWD, but we show a broad selection of types and sizes from around the world to give an idea of the main trends in the past twenty years.

The Belgian firm MOL was created in 1952 and from 1966 made complete special-purpose vehicles that normally employed Deutz air-cooled engines. We show a selection here from the earliest days of the firm up to the present time, when it had expanded to employ a workforce of 650 at its Hooglede and associated factories.

One of the original MOLs was this conversion of an International for oilfield use.

An early Deutz powered MOL 6 x 6 showing a marked likeness to a Magirus Deutz.

This 8 x 8 crane carrier chassis dates from the early 1970s.

A special 6 x 6 for oil exploration.

This 1972 MOL Buggy had a 110 bhp Deutz six-cylinder diesel, Bedford gearbox, Commer transfer box and Austin axles.

In the 1980s MOL offered Buggies with rigid or articulating frames and 4 x 4 or 6 x 6.

Oshkosh gained a contract to supply several thousand 8 x 8 M977 trucks to the US Army for delivery by the end of 1987. These were rigid eight-wheelers whilst Oshkosh also offers a pivotting 8 x 8 Dragon Wagon, also known as the MK48. The front portion, containing a 445 bhp Detroit diesel and Allison automatic transmission, can be coupled within half an hour to differing rear bogies carrying a choice of wrecker, fifth wheel coupling or cargo body with materal handling crane. Loads of up to ten tons can be carried cross-country or eleven tons in the case of the rigid eight-wheelers with the same engine.

Daimler-Benz, KHD, Krupp, MAN and Rheinstahl collaborated to make a family of 4 x 4, 6 x 6, and 8 x 8 armoured amphibians. The 6 x 6 shown had a load capacity of two to three tons and was powered by a ten-cylinder Mercedes-Benz multi-fuel 390 bhp engine with ZF automatic torque converter transmission. Carrying fourteen men, it could achieve 90 km/h. A similar mechanical specification was used in a series of MAN and Mercedes-Benz soft skinned army trucks.

The Czechoslovakian Tatra concern makes an interesting range of 4 x 4, 6 x 6 and 8 x 8 vehicles with air-cooled engines, central backbone chassis and swing axle independent suspension. Some of these are supplied to Semex in West Germany for conversion into crane carriers and other special purpose machines. Shown is an 8 x 8 tree planter on a Semex 36270 chassis with 400 bhp engine. The spherical jaws can dig up a tree without disturbing the roots.

Off Road

Since the mid 1960s the Russian army has acquired thousands of 8 x 8 cargo trucks and missile carriers. This is an MAZ 543 which uses a downrated version of a V12 525 bhp diesel tank engine with torque converter transmission and weighs 17.5 tons. When used for missile transport the nose lies between the twin cabs, which are presumably fitted primarily to allow rapid engine exchange or servicing. Judging by the lifting rings, they also can be removed in a short time.

This 1982 Russian 6 x 6 is known as the Ural 4320 and is built by the Uralsky Motor Works at Miass. It has a payload of five tonnes and a 10.85 litre V8 206 bhp diesel with two range, five-speed part-sychromesh gearbox. It has a seven tonne winch, can climb thirty per cent grades and wade in water to a depth of 1.5 metres. Numerous other off-road military-type trucks are built in Russian factories, notably the Kraz 256 B1 6 x 6 and the GAZ-66 4 x 4.

Titan has been a West German manufacturer of special purpose vehicles since 1974. Mercedes-Benz components are chiefly used, including engines. In the case of this 6 x 6 tractor the turbo diesel is a 525 bhp V12 with eight-speed gearbox and torque converter. Gross vehicle weight without trailer is 34 tonnes. Other Titan tractors use Mercedes-Benz forward control cabs and have up to five axles and engines of up to 615 bhp. Titan also makes fire crash tender and tipper chassis as well as many other off-road types.

These Tucker Sno-Cats, made in Medford, Oregon, exhibit the three body styles available in 1976 on the 1500 Series. They had Chrysler V8 318 cu ins petrol engines and could have four or five-speed gearboxes. Each rubber track was 76 inches long and overall width eight feet. Sno-Cats weighed between 5,500 and 6,000 lbs. unladen and could carry 1,800 lbs. Tucker has been building snow vehicles for over sixty years and its Sno-Cats have been used on various polar expeditions. Somewhat similar vehicles but with single tracks on each side are made by Kassbohrer in Germany.

Above: **Amongst British firms Bedford has always been unusual in offering its own factory built 4 x 4s. Although it announced the termination of regular truck production in 1986 it continued to build off-road military types. Shown here are two of its M-type 4 x 4 vehicles in a civilian role in 1973. They employed the fixed cab of the TK model and were used by Luton Corporation for taking treated effluent to local farms. Larger Bedford 4 x 4 and 6 x 6 types are based on the TM model and can have Bedford, Cummins or Detroit diesels.**

Opposite page: **One of America's pioneer truck firms is Autocar, which after joining White in 1953 increasingly became its specialist vehicle division. In 1981 Volvo acquired White and Autocar and this drilling rig dates from that time. It is mounted on an 8 x 6 chassis with driven front axle. The Volvo White Truck Corporation now uses an assortment of American proprietary engines as well as Volvo units.**

Above: **Pivot-steer dumptrucks have become big business in the last decade. DJB of Peterlee, in Co. Durham, UK, claims to be the world's largest producer of the larger sizes, whilst BM-Volvo make the majority of the smaller types. Some of the six-wheel DJBs can carry over 50 tons, though shown here is a 4 x 4 24 tonner. All DJBs use Caterpillar engine and mechanical components. Production started in 1973 and the thousandth was sold in 1979 with around five hundred per year ever since.**

For maximum off-road traction on small vehicles several, like the Argocat, Yanmar, Privateer and Terranger, have adopted 8 x 8 drive with high flotation tyres. The 1978 Terranger shown has a 64 bhp Volkswagen engine and automatic gearbox and was made by Saboteur Vehicles of Vernham Dean, Andover, UK. It could carry 0.9 tonnes and was fully amphibious. Most of the structure was made of aluminium and up to 50 mph was possible on the road and 10 mph in water.

The German Federal Army, or Bunderswehr, was formed in 1956 and originally used much American and British equipment. However, from the 1970s most of its equipment came from local firms. The specialist in amphibious vehicles was H. W. Gehlen KG, Eisenwerke, Kaiserlautern, which made EWK 4 x 4 machines with Deutz air-cooled diesels from about 1967. Shown here is one used by the civil authorities for fire fighting and rescue work. Note the anchor and fold-down anti-splash panel at the front.

The upmarket Range-Rover with V8 engine was new in 1970. A 1975/6 example is shown here alongside an ingenious crop-spraying conversion of a Thwaites Alldrive 4 x 4. Thwaites make pivot-steer dumptrucks in Leamington Spa, Warwickshire, UK, typically of around five tons capacity. This conversion was the work of Malcolm Smith of Melbourne, Derbyshire and instead of pivot steering has a rigid frame with rigid axles that are swung around a centre point to steer. In this way crop damage is minimised.

Above: All-wheel drive transporters for farming and forestry in mountainous regions are made by several firms in the countries bordering the Alps. This one is a Reform Muli made in Wels, Austria, and versions can have Perkins three-cylinder or Deutz two-cylinder diesels. Up to 3.4 tonnes can be carried including the weight of the special hay pick-up mechanism on this example. Mulis have eight forward and eight reverse gears and can climb sixty per cent gradients.

Opposite page top: Whilst Hotchkiss disappeared from the vehicle scene in the early 1970s and Latil changed ownership, there were still Citroen and Saviem offering medium weight 4 x 4s and a continuation of the old established Panhard business making armoured vehicles. Two newcomers to the French off-road scene were the Jeep type Cournil in 1960 and the larger ALM which first appeared in 1958. Shown is an early 1980s ALM VLRA 6 x 6 type TPK 6.42 SM2. It was for 4.3 tonne loads and had a 138 CV Perkins diesel and two range five-speed gearbox. It could wade in 0.9 metres of water, attain 85 km/h and was sold to 26 countries in addition to the French army. The example here is laying a temporary road.

Opposite page bottom: In the mid 1980s Foden and Scammell won large orders for medium and high mobility container carrying DROPS vehicles. Prior to that both firms had supplied large numbers of 6 x 4, 6 x 6, 8 x 4 and 8 x 6 trucks to NATO. Shown is a Foden with Rolls-Royce diesel. The Foden business was acquired by PACCAR, makers of Kenworth and Peterbilt in America, in 1980 and up to March 1987 had sold 4,500 vehicles, many of them for off-road use.

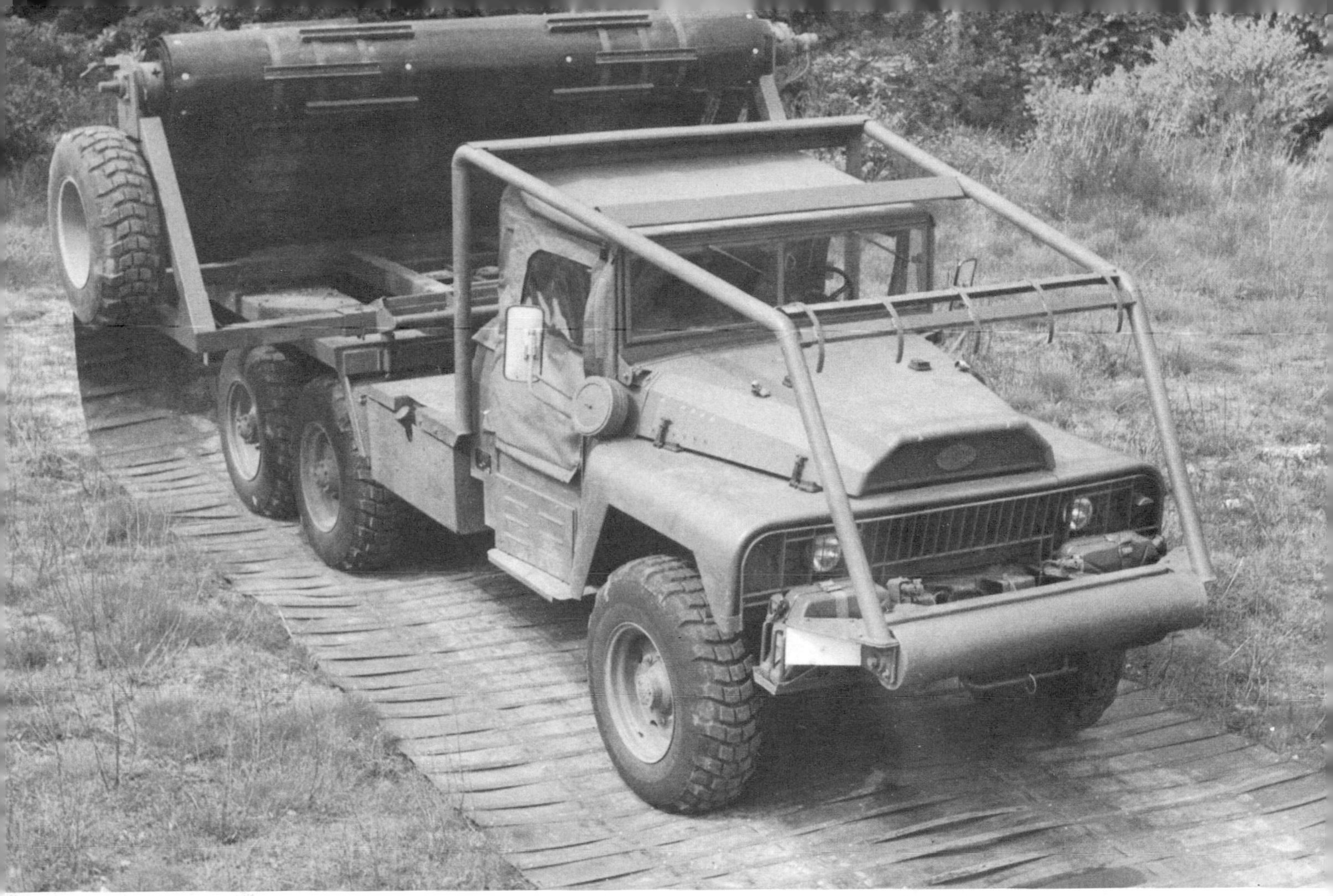

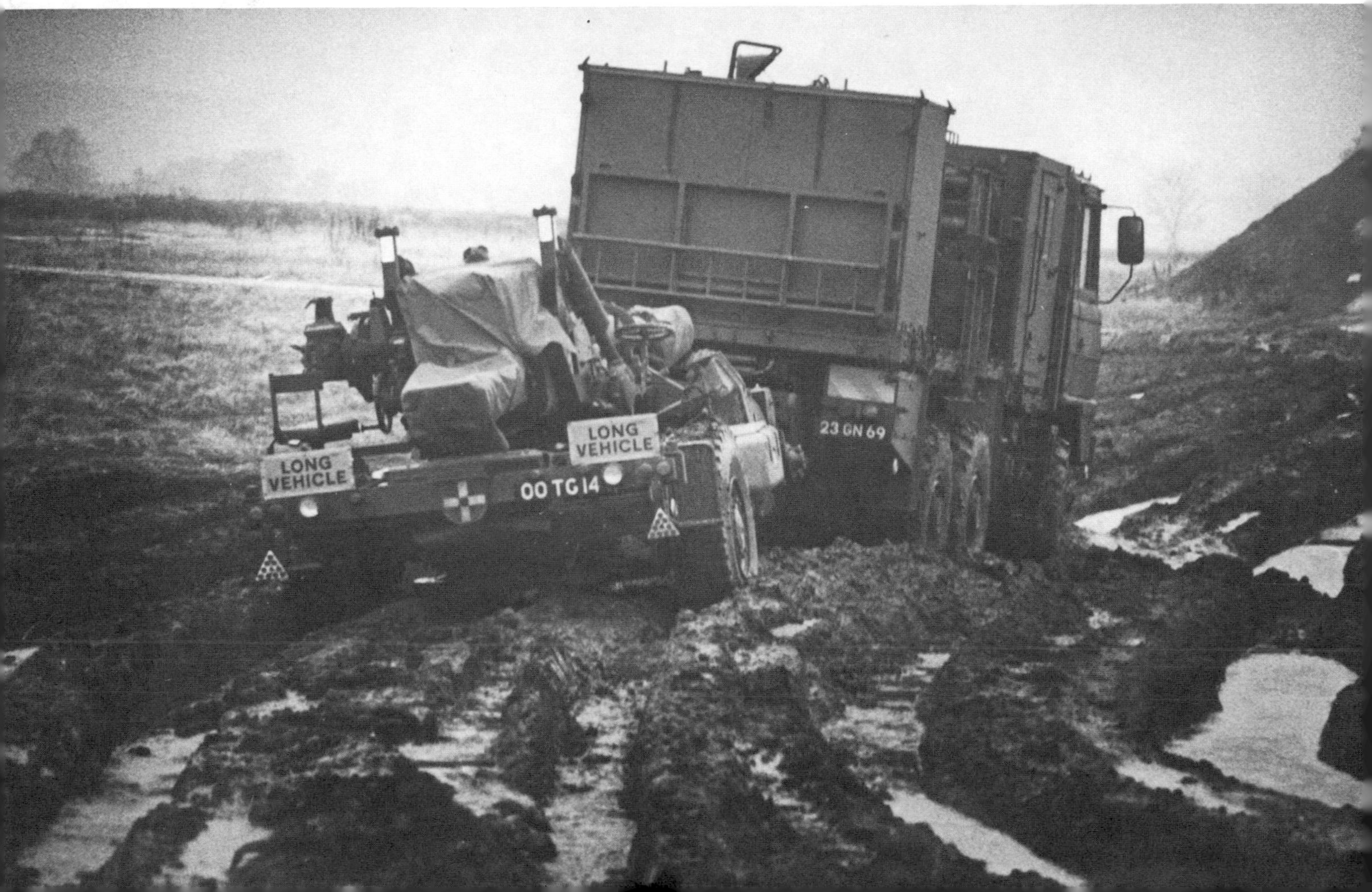
23 GN 69
LONG VEHICLE
LONG VEHICLE
00 TG 14

Opposite page: As part of a rugged, no frills export range, DAF built this six-wheeler 2800 bonnetted tractive unit in 1985. It had an 11.6 litre six-cylinder DAF engine available normally aspirated delivering 230 bhp or, with different turbocharger arrangements, up to 333 bhp. Leyland, with whom DAF merged in 1987, makes a similar series of strong and basic vehicles for undeveloped countries.

Above: Numerous firms make special logging vehicles in Scandinavia. The one here is a Volvo BM Valmet 886K built in 1982. It had a six-cylinder Volvo 125 kW diesel and Clark torque converter transmission with 6 x 6. Other versions can not only load timber, as in this case, but also fell it and strip it of branches without manual effort. Valmet is a Finnish firm acquired in recent years by Volvo BM. Note the lamps on the side to illuminate loading during the long sub-arctic winter.

Off Road

The Stonefield was developed from 1974 in Scotland and was the brainchild of haulage man Jim McKelvie, who had introduced Volvo trucks to Britain. 4 x 4, 6 x 4 and 6 x 6 versions were offered and a 1979/80 emergency tender used by Lothian and Borders Fire Brigade is shown. The vehicle was built around a robust space-frame and engines that could be installed included Ford and Chrysler with the Ferguson positive traction system embodied in the transmission. Stonefield joined the export-orientated Gomba group, but in the mid 1980s became independent and the factory was transferred to Strood, Kent, where Perkins diesels or Chrysler 5.2 litre petrol V8s were specified for its two to three tonne capacity vehicles.

A forward control 1½ ton capacity version of the Land-Rover appeared in 1962 incorporating virtually all the same parts as found in the long wheelbase conventional model. To gain greater stability, wider axles were later fitted and then in 1971 came this completely new military version that incorporated the V8 engine and other features of the Range-Rover. The Military 101″ shown here is working with a powered axle trailer driven off the Land-Rover's power take off. Land-Rover production reached a 1970s peak in 1975, when 58,000 were produced.

Above and right:

The Japanese involvement with light 4 x 4 vehicles had become important since Nissan and Toyota introduced their Patrol and Land-Cruiser vehicles in the early 1950s, and Mitsubishi acquired a Jeep licence in 1953. In the 1970s Japanese firms developed an untapped market for smaller, lighter vehicles of use to farmers, but cheap enough to be "second cars" for leisure motoring. Shown here is Subaru's 1600 4WD of 1978 looking like a conventional 4 x 2 pick-up and a 1984 Suzuki SJ410 with diminutive overhead camshaft 45 bhp petrol engine.

Off Road

Burgeoning demand for pivot-steered dumptrucks saw the arrival of Moxy vehicles in Norway in 1972 and some 2,000 were in use by 1987. Brown Engineering of Pool in Wharfedale, Yorkshire, UK, acquired the business and now builds some Ford engined models in the UK. The rest have Scania diesels including the 7235S shown here, which is a 412 bhp, 35 tonne capacity machine with ZF torque converter transmission and 6 x 6.

Reynolds Boughton of Amersham, Bucks, UK, makes 5 tonne GVW 4 x 4 RB44 vehicles. They used the Ford A series cab to begin with (as shown here) but with the demise of that model switched to the Dodge 50 cab in the 1980s. Various engines can be specified including Ford, Bedford and Perkins with manual or automatic transmission. The one here has a Ford V6 petrol engine and manual transmission providing eight forward speeds and POWR-Lok differentials.

Below and right:

Resembling the Auto-Union Munga was the VW Iltis shown here in the mid 1970s. VW had acquired Auto-Union in 1964 and the Munga continued to 1968, by when roughly 55,000 had been built. The Munga was a 4 x 4 developed in the mid 1950s for the Bundeswehr whilst the VW was introduced in 1969 as the 181 model for the same customer and had rear engine and rear-wheel drive. It looked similar to the 4 x 2 VW Kubelwagen of the Second World War. In the 1980s Bombardier of Canada acquired world rights to the Iltis and added it to its range of 6 x 6 lorries and tracked vehicles (the latter having been made since 1935). VW itself continues to make a light 4 x 4 in the shape of its Transporter (right) re-engineered by Steyr who had earlier made a success of its own diminutive Hafflinger 4 x 4 and now also does 4 x 4 work for FIAT and Mercedes-Benz.

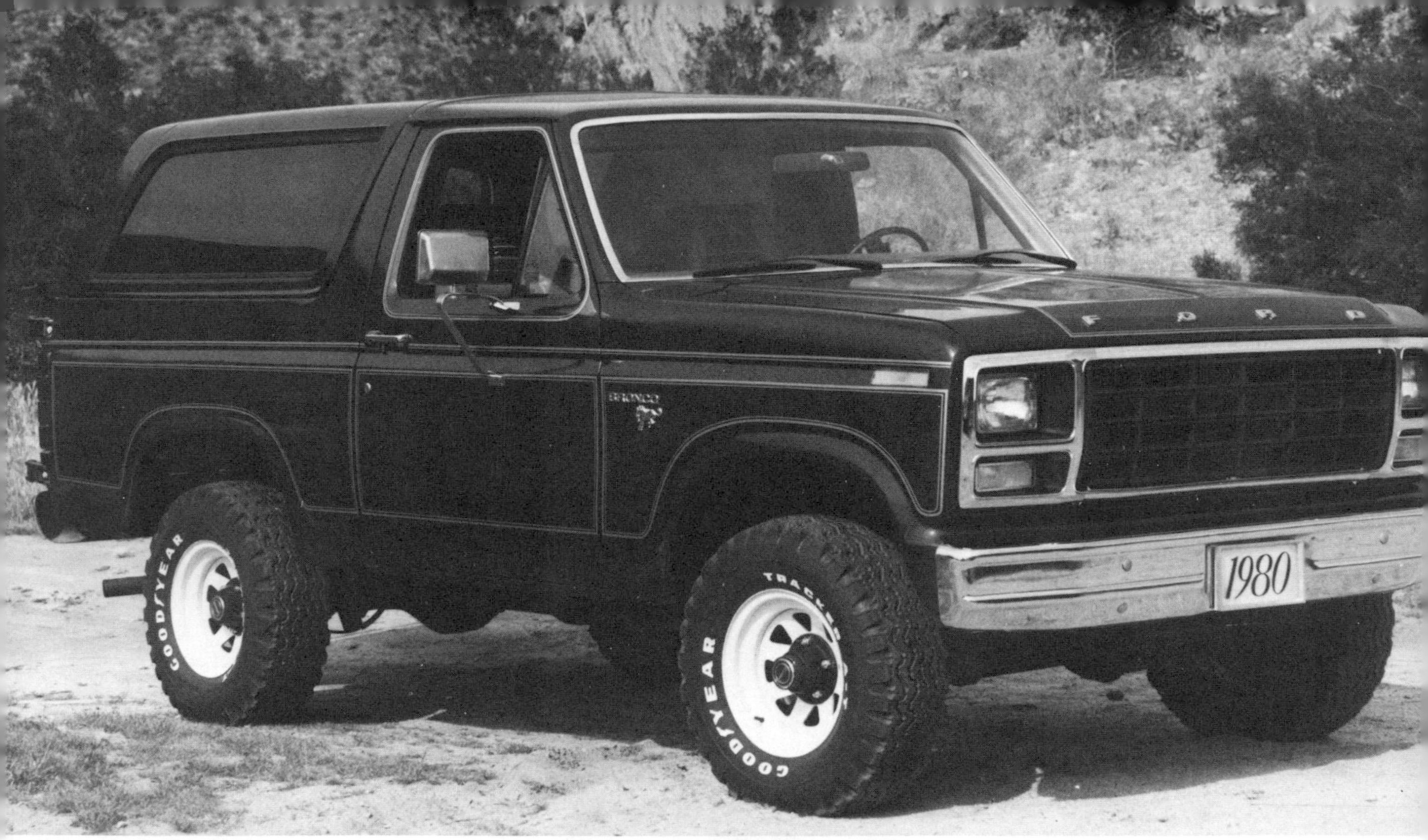
FORD
BRONCO
1980
GOODYEAR
TRACKER
GOODYEAR

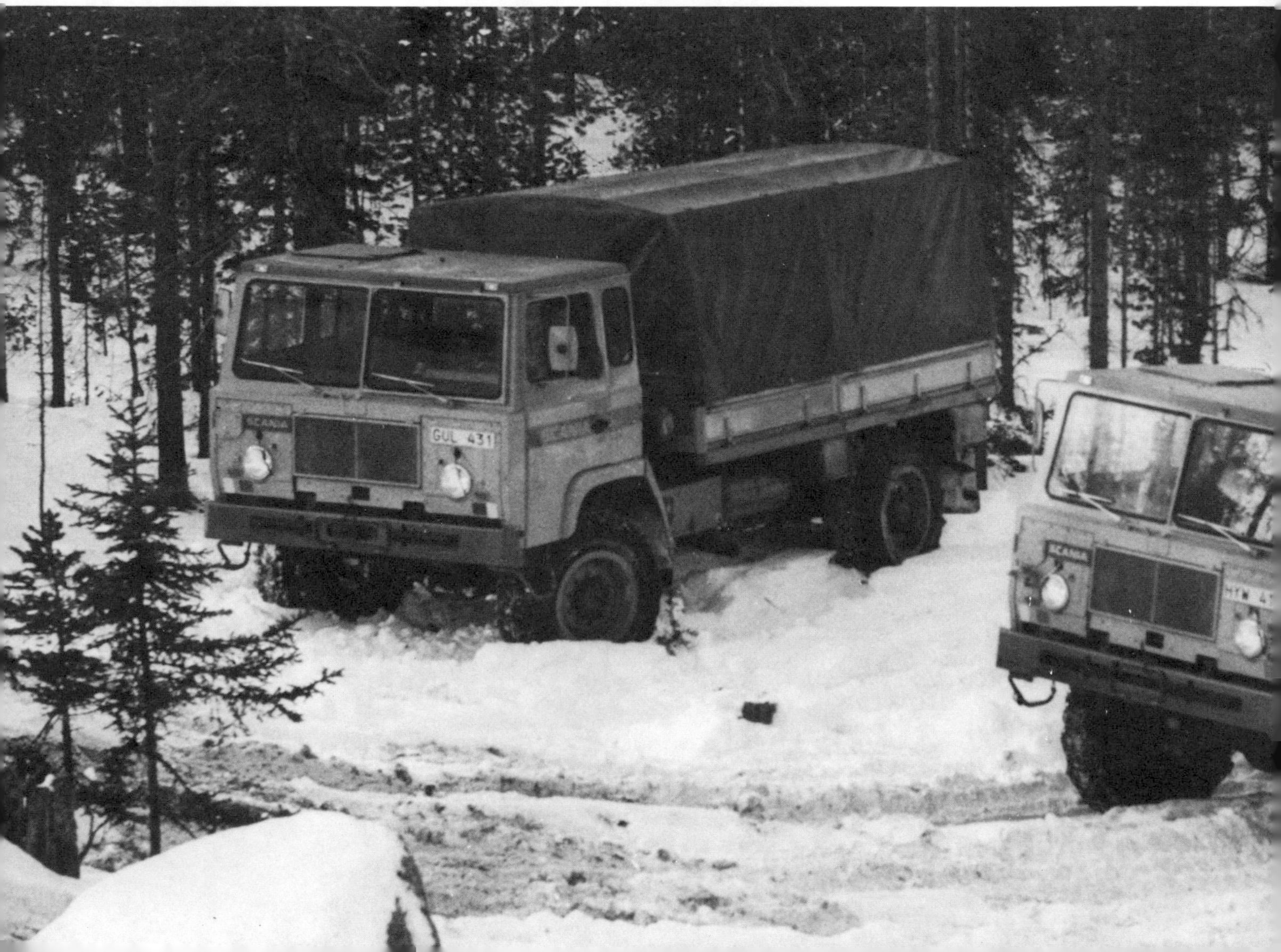
SCANIA
GUL 431

Off Road

Opposite page top:
One tends to think of the Jeep when thinking of light American 4 x 4s. However, they are by no means alone in the field and Ford, GMC, Dodge and International all make competing vehicles. This is the Ford Bronco of 1980, by when nearly 100,000 per year were being sold. Unlike earlier versions it had independent front suspension and could have six-cylinder or V8 petrol engines and manual or automatic transmissions.

This page top:
The Mercedes-Benz Gelandewagen (1980 example shown, when engines of 72 to 150 bhp were offered) was built by Steyr in Austria, who also make VW and FIAT 4 x 4 vehicles as well as its own range of large 4 x 4 and 6 x 6 trucks. The Gelandewagen, like the latest Land-Rovers, has beam axles with coil spring suspension and is available with hard or soft top and with or without rear side windows.

Left:
Scania's new military range of the mid 1970s consisted of the SBA111 4 x 4 and SBAT 111S 6 x 6. They had capacities of 4.5 and 6 tonnes and could respectively tow six and twelve tonne GVW trailers. They had hydraulic-mechanical automatic transmission (with a facility for being tow-started) and a D11 six-cylinder engine in the smaller truck with a turbocharged version in the larger. Parts commonality between the two types was around ninety per cent.

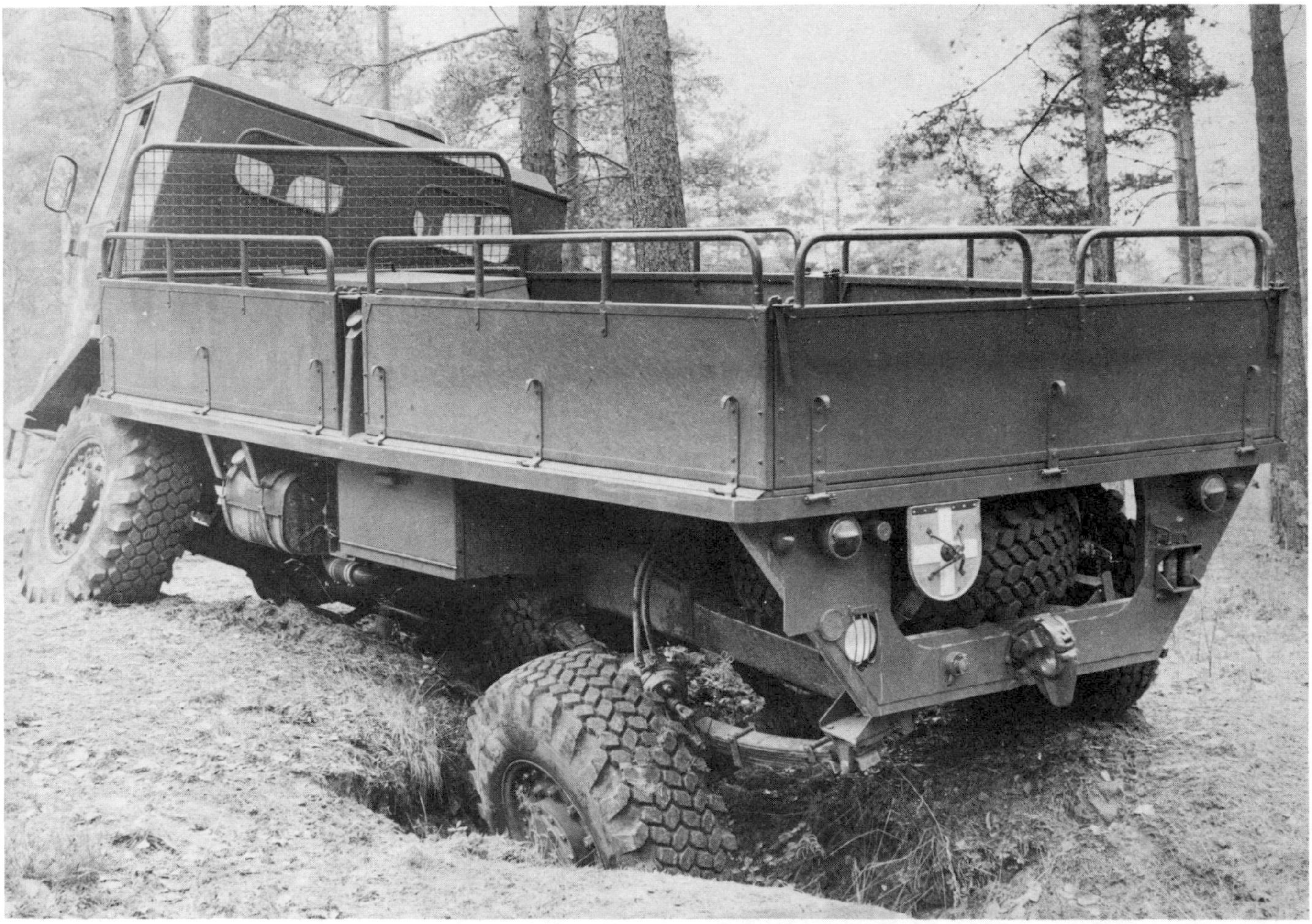

The Finnish truck manufacturer Sisu introduced its A-45/KB-45 4 x 4 in 1965 and went on to add 6 x 6 versions. An interesting feature of all was the ability to work with powered axle trailers. We have already encountered one of these in connection with the military 101″ Land-Rover, but the Sisu used hydrostatic wheel motors on its trailers and these same motors could also be applied to gun wheels and other equipment. The A-45 shown had a Leyland 0.410 diesel and, when equipped with hydrostatic trailer, was known as the Two-in-One.

As well as making tracked vehicles, Canadian Foremost produces two, three and four axle high flotation vehicles on giant pneumatic tyres. This is its Delta 3 for 15 ton loads. It can have Detroit or Cummins diesels of approximately 200 bhp output with Clark torque converter transmission. It steers by pivoting in the centre of the frame. The largest version with five man cab is 38′ 3″ (11.66 metres) long and fully laden the vehicle exerts a ground pressure of only sixteen pounds per square inch (110 kPa).

Brimont is the successor to the old French Latil, and like it, drives and steers on four wheels. Its 12.5 tonne GVW ETR model is also assembled in Kansas by the Ottawa Truck Corp, a firm which specialises in tugs and trailer spotters. The Commando uses a 171 bhp Renault engine as used in Renault trucks marketed as Mack Mid-Liners in America. It has a two range six-speed gearbox and frame that can oscillate fifteen degrees between the axles. The ability to crab-track is shown in this photograph.

The International Pay Hauler 180 was an interesting vehicle from the early 1970s. As can be seen, it featured twin tyres at front and rear to permit equalised weight distribution. It had 4 x 4 to minimise damage to haul roads or for loose surfaces and could have 456 to 560 bhp Cummins or Detroit engines and Twin Disc powershift transmission. Payload was up to fifty tons. Different versions were subsequently made before the dumptruck division was sold off by International Harvester as a separate company in the 1980s.

This large 8 x 8 machine is offered by IRTEX and TMU. The former initials derive from Ingéniére et Réalisations de Transports Exceptionels, a French company where Réne Harvey, formerly of Willème/PRP makes specialist vehicles. The TMU initials are those of Tomas Mintegui Uriguen of Bilbao, Spain, who also makes a forestry 6 x 6 with Pegaso 200 bhp diesel. The 8 x 8 PE shown has Soma axles, DAF cab, ZF transmission and Mercedes-Benz 430 bhp diesel. Picture by courtesy of Speciaal Transport Magazine of 7401 JC Deventer, Holland.

Amongst a wide range of West German 4 x 4, 6 x 6 and 8 x 8 trucks Faun offered the HZ 50.45/50 in 1981. Normal control 8 x 8s are, of course, unusual, this one having a GVW of fifty tonnes and a GTW of up to three hundred tons. Power was provided by a 455 bhp Deutz diesel (Cummins optional) with ZF gearbox. Transfer box and axles were by Faun, who also offer forward control versions of similar 8 x 8s.

Right and below:

4 x 4 versions of standard trucks continued to be made by numerous manufacturers around the world. This is a Spanish Ebro with Ignacio Palacios front axle. Palacios also made the Italian Selene axles for tractors under licence in Spain. Ebro also made Jeeps under licence at the time, with Perkins engines, under the name Bravo. In 1980 Nissan took control of Ebro, which had at one time made British Fords.

One of the most widely used heavy duty 6 x 6 trucks of the era has been the Magirus-Deutz (now called Iveco). Shown is a 1979 310 D 26 AK being used to water acacia seedlings in an effort to reclaim tracts of desert in Libya. The air-cooled Deutz engines appear to thrive in the heat of the Sahara and equally on a major pipeline project employing hundreds of Ivecos in Siberia.

Australia's indigenous make of off-road and special purpose vehicles since 1969 has been R. F. Whitehead's RFW Truck Mfg. Corp. of Chester Hill, NSW. Amongst the current range are 4 x 4 and 6 x 6 crash tender and bush fire chassis. The strange machine depicted is an emergency vehicle that can cross difficult terrain to reach a railway line and then lower its flanged wheels and propel itself by contact between the tyres and rails. RFW offers Caterpillar, Cummins and Detroit engines.

In the early 1980s the Dutch firm of Terberg at Benschop was making about 350 special-purpose vehicles per year, many of them for off-road use. This 8 x 8 pipe carrier was one of five supplied to Algeria, where each carried six 24 metre lengths weighing up to 45 tonnes. They had Volvo 12 litre 350 bhp turbo diesels with torque converter transmissions. All eight wheels were steerable on their Kessler axles. Unladen height was only 2.3 metres and length was adjustable between 13.7 and 18.6 metres.

The old-established French Willème firm had made some giant all-wheel driven vehicles in the 1950s and 1960s. When they ceased production around 1970 a licence to use some of their designs and their name was acquired by special purpose vehicle maker Perez & Raimond Paris (PRP) of Villeneuve la Garenne. Shown is a 1975 oilfield truck with Detroit 318 bhp diesel, Allison automatic gearbox and Willème double reduction axles. Some Willème heavy haulage designs ultimately went to MOL in Belgium.

Above: In Japan, Nissan, Mitsubishi and Hino all produce heavy duty off-road vehicles and these have had considerable export success in the Far East and Africa. The 4 x 4 Nissan Diesel UD loggers have 300 bhp V8 diesel and choice of various Nissan and Fuller transmission options. Forward and normal control 4 x 4 and 6 x 6 versions are also offered as dumptrucks, crane carriers and military vehicles.

Right:

Walter, whose earlier products we have already considered, nowadays makes mostly crash tender and snow plough chassis. This is its latest styling on normal control or conventional trucks, as they are called in America. Various engine and transmission options are offered, but drive continues to be to ring gears in the wheel hubs leaving the axle beams with nothing but load carrying, spring mounting and steering duties. This gives greater ground clearance than a normal axle with banjo for input drive and differential.

Photographs on this and previous page: **Kenworth** had been a major producer of oilfield trucks ever since its acquisition by Pacific Car and Foundry in 1945. The 953 model shown here with a massive forty ton Holmes wrecker on its bed and representatives of Kenworth and Holmes in the foreground, can have Caterpillar, Cummins or Detroit engines of 304 to 456 bhp. The C500 6 x 6 is one of a series of Brute models, which first appeared in 1973. The Brute is also widely used in forestry and the construction industry. The driver receiving instructions to turn second right at the Kasbah is in charge of a 311 6 x 6 model.